LIBRARIES OF THE INFORMATION ERA

LIBRARIES OF THE INFORMATION ERA

Anand Ballabh

ACE BOOKS INDIA
NEW DELHI

ACE Books India
4649-B/21, Ansari Road
Darya Ganj, New Delhi - 110 002

Libraries of the Information ERA

First Published 2010
ISBN 978-81-909743-3-2

Sole Distributors
EKTA BOOKS DISTRIBUTORS
4649-B/21, Ansari Road
Darya Ganj, New Delhi - 110 002
Ph.: 23263193 / 9811582579 / 09435116718
Fax: 011-23263193
Email: ektabooks@yahoo.com
www.akanshapublishinghouse.com

PRINTED IN INDIA

Published by ACE Books India, New Delhi and Printed at Harmain Offset Press

Contents

PREFACE

"One of the saddest things about human nature is, that a man may guide others in the path of life, without walking in it himself; that he may be a pilot, and yet a castaway."

The libraries of information era are popularly known as digital or electronic libraries. Here will discuss some salient features of digital libraries in pros and cons.

The idea of easy, finger-tip access to information-what we conceptualize as digital libraries today-began with Vannenar Bush's Memex machine and has continued to evolve with each advance in information technology. With the arrival of computers, the concept centered on large bibliographic databases, the now familiar online retrieval and public access systems that are part of any contemporary library.

When computers were connected into large networks forming the Internet, the concept evolved again, and research turned to creating libraries of digital information that could be accessed by anyone from anywhere in the world. Phrases like "virtual library," "electronic library," "library without walls" and, most recently, "digital library," all have been used interchangeably to describe this broad concept. But what does this phrase mean? What is digital library? And what are the issues and challenges in creating them? Moreover, what are the issues involved in creating a coordinated scheme of digital libraries? It has been suggested that digital libraries will only be viable within such a scheme. Here we have ried to address these questions.

In fact, 'Information' in electronic digital form is both enabling and complicating. On the one hand, electronic digital information is more accessible - available from anywhere in the world with a few computer keystrokes or mouse clicks. On the other hand, it is less accessible because it is not directly perceivable to humans unaided by technology. We are dependent on machines to express this information in forms that we can perceive. Electronic digital information is manipulable - it allows us to use the computational power of computers systematically to aggregate, classify, compare, change, and transmit information. Electronic digital information forms allow copies to be made perfectly and recursively.

As is suggested from the name of title, here we intend to aelucidate various crucial issues, salient features and advantages of the modern libraries of present day. Judiciously selected and succinct information is gathered under the following main headings—Introduction; Online Information Retrieval; Digital Library: Elements, Concepts and Scope; Automation and Data Collection Management; Main Elements of Electronic Libraries; Computer-Based Acquisitions System and Relevant Issues; Glossary; and Bibliography etc.

Definitely, the contents will enlighten and delight academics as well as professional at various levels in the field of library and information science.

WIth the sole aim of furnishing authentic and latest information to the users of this book, we have tried our best by subscribing the views and works of different authorities in the field. Information is supported by facts and figures derived from various sources e.g. books, professional magazines and journals and relevant web sources. I express my gratitude to them all. While working on this project I was immensely benefitted by the guidance, assistance and inspiration extended by my seniors, colleagues and family members. I am grateful to them all. Finally, I am thankful to my publishers for undertaking publication of this book.

—AB

1

INTRODUCTION

"Where is the wisdom we have lost in knowledge?
Where is the knowledge we have lost in information?"

—T.S. Eliot, *The Rock*

In popular parlance, our current age is known as the Information era. Information and communication technology (ICT) has brought great revolution in all spheres. Now we live in a knowledge society.

Here it is important to note that before proceeding to library and information science of information era, first we must acquaint with information, information seeking and various techniques being used for it.

Information is a valuable resource in an information society; thus acquiring and using information are critical activities. The process known as information seeking is therefore becoming more fundamental and strategic for intelligent citizenship. In addition, the information-seeking process is more and more dependent on electronic technology. Here we examine the physical, cognitive, and affective consequences of electronic environments on the increasingly important process of information seeking and provides a framework for designing systems that support information seeking. It takes the point of view that information seeking depends on the interactions among information seekers and other people and systems for representing information. It argues that highly interactive electronic information systems are causing incremental changes in how we seek, acquire, and use information. The high volume and diverse forms of information demand better tools, which in turn change our behaviors, expectations, and attitudes. At this stage in the evolution of the information society, we need designs that place users in control of highly interactive environments that focus on content rather than on forms and tools.

What is Information?

First it is remarkable to quote Buckland (1991) who distinguished information-as-process (the communication act), information-as-knowledge (an increase or reduction in uncertainty), and information-as-thing (the objects that may impart information). In this vein, he also distinguished the actual knowledge in a human mind (what one knows) from the artifacts of the world that represent knowledge. Most generally, *information* is anything that can change a person's knowledge. This sense, according to Belkin (1978), admits reflection on one's memory traces, the objects that convey information, and the ideas and knowledge contained in other minds. Thus, information is used in this book in a general manner that includes objects in the world, what is transferred from people or objects to a person's cognitive system, and as the components of internal knowledge in people's minds. To seek information, people seek to change the state of their knowledge and also physical representations (e.g., ink on paper, sound waves, electronically charged phosphorus) that represent abstractions (e.g., words, numbers, images, concepts, melodies) that can cause this change. Because there are many manifestations of information-as-object, there are many terms that can be used to describe those objects.

Terms such as bit, data, record, text fragment, graphic, document, utterance, database, book, and library all are used to label particular information units. Although these terms are typically associated with different media or information systems, the terms *document* and *information object* are used herein in a general way to represent information-as-object. Thus, documents may be considered as a single numeric value, a database record, a distinct image, or a video segment, as well as the more typical textual collection of words related to a topic.

What is Information Seeking?

In fact, much of human existence is characterised by the notion of search; we seek and pursue material objects such as food or shelter, sensual experiences such as adventure or ceremony, and ethereal objects such as knowledge or justice. We are concerned here with the search for information that we will call *information seeking,* a process in which humans purposefully engage in order to change their state of knowledge. The term *search* is used to mean the behavioral manifestation of humans engaged in information seeking and also to describe the actions taken by computers to match and display information objects.

The term *information seeking* is preferred to *information retrieval* because it is more human oriented and open-ended. Retrieval implies that the object must have been "known" at some point; most often, those people who "knew" it organised it for later "knowing" by themselves or someone else. Seeking connotes the process of acquiring knowledge; it is more problem oriented as the solution may or may not be found. For example, seeking spiritual enlightenment makes sense, but retrieving enlightenment does not. Retrieval is applicable to database management and most applied problems, but seeking is closer to answering questions or learning. Information seeking is a fundamental human process closely related to learning and problem solving. Nature has evolved tools and methods to support information seeking, resulting in physiological and psychological abilities that are well suited to information seeking.

Our perceptual organs gather massive streams of environmental data; our muscles aim these organs and carry us closer to the objects of search; and our cognitive and emotive engines direct muscles and organs and process the incoming data. Our cognitive processors adopt various organisational structures and systematic strategies for filtering, comparing, and storing information in a variety of media.

Our emotive selves derive stimulation and pleasure from seeking and integrating information. Information seeking is thus a natural and necessary mechanism of human existence. The information-seeking processes needed to survive and prosper have become more complex as social organisations have developed. The ability to locate and apply information is an important component of what it means to be literate. Just as nature has evolved physiological and psychological tools and methods to support information seeking, so culture has evolved tools and methods to support information seeking. Information-processing technologies from the abacus to the zoetrope help us generate, manipulate, and represent information. As social and economic organisations have become more complex, so has the information necessary to work in these organisations, and this has led to new, more powerful technologies for managing information.

Today, the generation, storage, and communication of information are inextricably linked with technology - it is virtually impossible to conduct business in many markets today without technology to help manage the generation, storage, and flow of information. Likewise, an enormous amount of information is necessary to select from entertainment options and to make good consumer decisions. Thus, one of the key changes in the information society is that information seeking has become a fundamental skill for larger portions of the population - more people must regularly manage more information in order to survive and prosper and they must use an expanding array of technologies to do so. Information seeking, like learning, is a fundamental and high level cognitive process. Information seeking is often part of learning or problem solving, but it is also distinct. Information acquired during learning is stored so that it can be recalled and used at a later time, although information acquired as a result of information seeking may be useful for a specific task and then discarded. Intermediate or temporally relevant information often should be discarded so that it does not take up storage space or complicate the organisation of stored information and subsequently interfere with retrieval functions. Information seeking at the level of scientific research is accumulative, with each new finding supporting or questioning theories and principles. Information seeking at the operational level often uses the results quickly and directly, archiving or discarding the information as soon as it is applied rather than making it part of the corporate memory.

Because humans cannot selectively erase their memories, much of the information processed as part of information seeking is remembered, regardless of whether we think we will ever use it again. As we depend more on the external augmentation of our memories, especially through electronic technology, we should decide whether and how to store information. We must consider information from a life-cycle perspective in which destruction options are developed along with generation, acquisition, and storage options. As we seek, evaluate, and acquire information, we must consider integratability with respect to our existing private or corporate knowledge and reusability for future problems. Technology can surely help us be more selective about what information we store and thus use our mental and external resources better, but we must balance optimisation against our abilities to spout trivia at parties or make disparate connections that spark intellectual breakthroughs. Learning takes place in directed and incidental ways, but information seeking as defined here is a directed (purposeful) activity. There are, however, two ways that information can be acquired incidentally. First, our physical survival depends on our senses' constantly gathering information about the environment to alert us to dangers and possible gratifications. This kind of automatic search for information is important to survival but is beyond the scope of our definition of information seeking. Second, as we purposely seek information, we encounter many prospective units of information that we filter and compare. We remember much of this irrelevant information automatically in spite of our efforts to ignore it, and so we should be concerned with ways to minimise and label such information. The focus of this book is on intentional information seeking, a process driven by an information problem.

The information problem can be a mild curiosity, the desire to occupy 30 minutes, an ongoing passion about a hobby, or a desperate quest with life-critical consequences, but it must initiate a conscious activity to move toward a goal. As with learning or problem solving, we develop strategies to guide our progress. We use a variety of gross strategies in information seeking, including consulting our own long-term memory; asking friends, colleagues, or experts; consulting personal collections of books, periodicals, and files; conducting empirical investigations; and applying formal systems.

Formal systems include libraries, research firms, government agencies, electronic networks, and the growing collection of information services that make up the information industry. The main focus here is on information seeking using formal systems, although as we shall see in later chapters, electronic technologies are blurring the distinctions among personal, informal, and formal information systems. In addition to strategies defined by what sources are used for search, there are strategies for how one should search. A fundamental distinction is made between analytical and browsing strategies (Liebscher & Marchionini, 1988; Marchionini & Shneiderman, 1988).

Analytical strategies depend on careful planning, the recall of query terms, and iterative query reformulations and examinations of results. *Browsing* strategies are heuristic and opportunistic and depend on recognising relevant information. Analytic strategies are batch oriented and half duplex (turn taking) like human conversation, whereas browsing strategies are more interactive, real-time exchanges and collaborations between the information seeker and the information system.

Browsing strategies demand a smaller cognitive load in advance and a steadier attentional load throughout the information-seeking process. Analytical strategies can be applied by intermediaries for the benefit of the person requesting information, whereas browsing strategies are conducted by the ultimate user of the information. In practice, people apply different mixes of analytical and browsing strategies, but electronic environments have severely limited what strategies information seekers can use. Although people have an inclination to browse, analytical strategies are more efficient in large document collections. Early computer systems required analytical strategies, and some present-day systems require browsing under the guise of ease of use.

Both these developments have influenced how we seek information, and this book distinguishes between these strategies and argues for a new generation of designs that support both strategies.

Information seeking is often a type of learning, because the goal in both cases is to change knowledge. Information seeking differs from learning according to the degree of retention desired; learning demands retention and information seeking may use the information for a temporary task. Much of information seeking may require identifying and retrieving previously stored information. Thus, information retrieval is one type of information seeking except when it is conducted by a machine - machines cannot seek information but they can retrieve information. Information may be retrieved by people in order to support learning. Browsing is often a type of learning and is not usually driven by well-defined goals or does not usually proceed according to a systematic plan as information retrieval does. Analytical search is sometimes a type of learning and is most closely associated with retrieval. As will be demonstrated when these strategies are characterised in later chapters, browsing and analytical search do have some similarities.

Our world continues to become increasingly complex, interconnected, and dynamic: There are more people and institutions; they engage in more relationships and exchange; and the rates of change continue to grow, largely because of developments in technology and the importance of information to human and technical development. We live in an information society in which more people must manage more information, which in turn requires more technological support, which both demands and creates more information.

Electronic technology and information are mutually reinforcing phenomena, and one of the key aspects of living in the information society is the growing level of interactions we have with this complex and increasingly electronic environment. The general consequences of the information society are threefold: larger volumes of information, new forms and aggregations of information, and new tools for working with information.

First, we find ourselves dealing with more information in all aspects of our lives. More of us are "knowledge workers," generating, managing, and communicating information to produce and provide goods and services for an increasingly global economy. In addition to the often-noted trend toward more people managing more information in the workplace, people must go beyond the workplace to learn new skills and acquire new knowledge to do their jobs. But new knowledge is no longer acquired only to prepare for a career but, rather, is now an essential part of "knowledge work." As Zuboff (1988, p. 395) noted, "To put it simply, learning is the new form of labor." Lifelong learning as part of the job has long been an important part of professional responsibilities and has spread to all venues of the labor force. More than 57 million adults participated in some form of adult education in 1990-91, of which almost 13 million were professionals *(Statistical Abstract of the United States 1993).*

Notably, these large volumes of information are organised into many collections that require secondary and tertiary indexes and directories that in turn are growing in size and complexity. The growth of directories and indexes is reflected in the competition among different companies that offer phone directories and bibliographic databases. The development of new and alternative organisational structures for dealing with large volumes of information in turn demands more information management skills. In our personal lives, billboards, newspapers, mail, telephone, and television serve as vehicles for the incessant information assaults on our senses. To cope with these large amounts of information in our lives, we have developed complex personal information infrastructures, which require time and effort to build, maintain, and use.

These structures include conscious and unconscious filtering and finding strategies for achieving our immediate goals and protecting ourselves from information overload. There is a tension between the goals and plans we make and the information resources necessary to achieve them; we travel a narrow road toward our goals with a sea of seductive information to distract us on one side and a spiraling abyss of confusion and information overload on the other. Technology accelerates the rate at which we are able to travel toward our goals, but it also increases the scope and peril of the two sides.

Second, we deal with information in new forms, especially electronic digital forms that are more abstract, more dynamic, and more malleable than is printed or painted information. Much more information is becoming available in electronic form.

In fact, 'Information' in electronic digital form is both enabling and complicating. On the one hand, electronic digital information is more accessible - available from anywhere in the world with a few computer keystrokes or mouse clicks. On the other hand, it is less accessible because it is not directly perceivable to humans unaided by technology. We are dependent on machines to express this information in forms that we can perceive. Electronic digital information is manipulable - it allows us to use the computational power of computers systematically to aggregate, classify, compare, change, and transmit information. Electronic digital information forms allow copies to be made perfectly and recursively, unlike analog or physical forms that degrade over generations of copies.

Electronic digital information is simple because it is fully expressed by only two elements (bits), but it is complex because many levels of coding schemes must be used to map the enormous variety of structure and meaning in the world into binary form. The many sets of codings necessary for humans to "make sense" out of digital information allows the same digital code to be represented in many ways; for example, the set of bits 1001101 can be expressed on a display as an uppercase "M" or as a set of black and white pixels in a larger image, or as part of a note value for a compact disk recording. Standard coding schemes (e.g., American Standard Code for Information Interchange - ASCII, Tag Image File Format - TIFF, Digital Alternative Representation of Musical Scores - DARMS) facilitate communication and exchange of information, but the many possibilities support a kind of information alchemy in which words, numbers, images, and sounds can be interchanged - for better or worse. Given the sound and graphic editing tools available, it is no longer possible to believe that digitally recorded sounds or images represent reality. The implication for humans is that additional levels of learning and cognitive-effort are necessary to use, interpret, and validate information based on electronic digital expressions.

Further, we find ourselves using new tools to manage information—tools that we must learn to use, pay for, and maintain. The primary tool of the information society is the computer. Microprocessors are used to improve the performance of other technologies, and computers are increasingly used to control and integrate other kinds of information technology (e.g., TV, radio, telephones). Computer literacy has become a component in primary and secondary school curricula in all industrialised countries, and billions of dollars a year are spent on training and upgrading workers' computer skills. As more computing technology is created, more new learning and retraining will be needed, placing demands on our time and financial resources.

The computer industry accounts for an increasingly large share of the gross national product of the industrialised countries, and the massive personal computer market has driven the invention of new software tools that fit the needs of a great variety of users. The need to produce products that can be used by the general population has in turn spurred advances in human-computer interface research. Although much progress has been made in making computers easier to use, the evolution of hardware and software and the rapid pace of information creation and manipulation mean that for the foreseeable future, significant material and intellectual resources must be devoted to acquiring, learning to use, applying, and maintaining electronic tools. At the very least, it is obvious that more and more of our time and financial resources must be spent using computers, and we will become even more dependent on them in the future. An important aspect of these effects is that more of our professional and personal lives will be spent interacting with complex systems. Interactions with other people are physiologically natural, psychologically necessary, and culturally expected. These interactions became increasingly mediated as communications technology developed, and computer technology is another step toward intermediated personal communication.

This trend is illustrated by use of electronic mail, which had 9.2 million users in 1992 and is projected to have 38 million users by 1995 (Reinhardt, 1993). Individual people also interact with a variety of institutional systems such as government agencies, businesses, and other organisations. These interactions were traditionally mediated by other people, but information technology is finding increasing application. Consider, for example, the automatic teller machines, phone menu systems, and information kiosks at shopping malls or museums.

As more of these systems are connected, many of our interactions with the institutions of civilisation and with other people will take place through electronic workstations rather than through personal contact. Working from one's workstation saves time and resources, and the computational power facilitates the execution of multiple tasks concurrently. The implications of mediated communication, high rates of exchange, and parallel processing of tasks are considered under the topic of interactivity.

2

Online Information Retrieval

In the preceding chapter we have elucidated information alongwith its salient features in the context of modern library and information science.

Here in this chapter we will highlight the online information retrieval which is crucial for modern libraries.

Basically, concept of using machines for storage and processing of information can be traced as far back as 1960's. In late 1960's online bibliographic databases were made available as a by-product of primary printed publications. The world's first computer produced periodical - *Chemical Titles* - was introduced by Chemical Abstracts Service (CAS) in 1961. It has covered 750 chemically oriented journals. Each article was indexed by author and keywords with a reference to the journal in which it has appeared. The computers were used for typesetting. Use of computers for typesetting made it possible to accommodate more material in a machine readable form.

The creation of machine readable databases helped in providing alerting services. This was beginning of a significant change in information retrieval. The machine readable databases were manipulated further to produce a variety of products such as indexes in printed forms for manual searching. The 1970's witnessed the extensive use of computers in information handling.

The creation of machine readable databases like Chemical Abstracts, Biological Abstracts, Index Medicus by secondary information services coincided with the development of long distance telecommunication networks like Tymnet and Telenet in USA. The online search concept as an industry started when two organisations viz. M/s. Lockheed under M/s. Dialog Information Services in 1972 and M/s System Development Corporation (SDC) in 1973 provided softwares and necessary computing facilities to enable the databases to be sorted and searched interactively in batch mode through telecommunication networks.

Information is a commercially exploitable commodity. It has to be produced/generated, communicated and used properly. It is "unscare" resource and continues to grow at an explosive rate.

The tasks of locating and communicating information presents the following problems:

(i) Large volume of information causes overload at the processing end.

(ii) Increasing time lag between generating and publishing information.

(iii) Interdisciplinary nature of growth in science possesses problems in locating the desired information.

(iv) Proliferation in the growth of primary and secondary journals presents problems in bibliographic control.

(v) Language and other communication barriers.

A vast array of electronic gadgets have been produced to store, organize and communicate the information world wide at a very fast speed. The rapid advancement in computers, storage media and software packages for processing information have eased the situation considerably. It has been possible to convert large volumes of information and data available in abstracting and indexing services in science and technology into machine readable from called databases. At present there are over 7000 such products available for commercial exploitation through over 600 vendors world wide.

Computerised Databases

Extensive use of computers for information storage and processing resulted in creation of computerised databases covering all area of science and technology. These databases are of two major varieties viz. (1) Reference Databases and (2) Source Databases. Reference databases are of two categories such as *(a)* Bibliographic and *(b)* Referral. Records in bibliographic databases contain clues to the intellectual content and physical characteristics of pieces of the graphic or printed record of humanity such as journal article, research report, conference proceedings, book or patent etc. The referral databases contain directory type information such as list of persons, organisations, research projects etc.

Source databases are primary sources of information or data composed of the full texts of the information in question and including materials prepared specifically for distribution by electronic means.

These databases could be further subdivided into (a) Full Text, (b) Numeric and (c) A combination of the two—textual numeric.

Full text database contain original textual material belonging to primary sources such as encyclopedia, newspaper, court decisions, journals etc.

Numeric database contains original numeric or statistical data such as financial, census, production trade data.

Textual numeric databases contains fields of mixed textual and numeric data and includes dictionary or handbooks.

Here it is pertinent to furnish information on some important databases in science and technology.

Reference Databases

Bibliographic Databases

(1) *Biosis Previews:* Producer: Biosciences Information Service, USA. Contains Over seven million records.1969 to present.

(2) *CA Search:* Producer: Chemical Abstracts Service, USA. Contain over nine million records. 1967 to present.

(3) *Compendex Plus:* Producer: Institute for Scientific Information (ISI), USA. Contain over two million records. 1970 to present.

Referral Databases

(1) *American Library Directory:* Producer: R.R. Bowker, USA. Contain over thirty six thousand records. Current.

(2) *American men and Women of Science:* Producer: R.R. Bowker, USA Contains over one lakh records. Current.

(3) *Books In Print:* Producer: Thomas Publishing Company Inc., USA. Contains over one lakh fifty thousand records. Current.

Source Databases

Fulltext Databases

(1) *Harvard Business Review:* Producer: John Wiley & Sons Inc., USA. Contains over two thousand five hundred records. 1971 to present.

(2) *Kirk Othmer Online:* Producer: Wiley Electronic Publishing, USA. Contains over thirty three thousand records. 3rd Edition.

(3) *Martindale Online:* Producer: The Pharmaceutical Society

of Great Britain, UK. Over forty three thousand records. Current edition.

(4) *PTS Newsletter Database:* Producer: Predicast, USA. Contains over four lakh records. January 1988 to present.

Numeric Databases

(1) *Cendata:* Producer: US Bureau of the Census, USA. Contains over fifty two thousand records current.

(2) *Mediai General Plus:* Producer: Media General Financial Services Inc., USA Contains over seven thousand records. Current.

(3) *D&B Donneley Demographies:* Producer: Donnelley Marketing Services, USA Contains over sixty two thousand records. Current.

(4) *D&B Duns Financial Records Plus:* Producer: Duns and Bradstreet Credit Services, USA Contains over Twenty lakh records. Current.

Textual/Numeric Databases

(1) *ICC International Annual Reports:* Producer: ICC Online Ltd. UK, contains over ninety seven thousand records. Current.

(2) *Extel International News Cards:* Producer: Extel Financial Ltd. UK. Contains over twenty one thousand records. October 1989 to present.

(3) *Investext:* Producer: Technical Data International Inc., USA. Contains over fourteen lakh records. July 1982 to present.

(4) *Moody's Corporate News:* Producer: Moody's Investor Services Inc., USA. Contains over three lakh seventy thousand records, 1988 to present.

TELESEARCHING

Telecommunication Modes

Since 1970 there have been considerable growth in the production of computer readable databases. As on today there are over seven thousand publically available machine readable databases as compared to few hundreds at the beginning. These are marketed through over eight hundred search services providers popularly known as vendors. Improvements in telecommunication system, satellite links and modems transmitting at 2400 baud or higher speeds are commonly used for online searching. The advancements in computer technology and telecommunication systems have also brought down the searching costs considerably.

In case of India, the following are the three modes of telecommunication available for accessing computerised databases:

1. Telex Mode

Most of the institutes/organisations possess a telex terminal as a means of communication. This system can be used for conducting online searches too. Advancements in telex machines from electrical telex to computerized Message Communication Terminals (MCT) to PC Telex cards have made the transmission more easy. The transmission speed of this system is 50 bauds per seconds. This slow speed makes online searching more costlier as compared to other modes.

2. Dialup Data Service (PSTN)

Under this mode two computers are connected through telephone lines to transmit data. It is called Dialup Data Service (PSTN). Here modems to inter phase the computer and telephones lines are used at both the ends. The speed of transmission are 300 or 1200 bauds.

3. GPSS/PAD Mode

With the introduction of Gateway Packet Switching Service

(GPSS)and Packet Assembler Disassembler (PAD), data can be transmitted at a rate of 1200 bauds, 2400 bauds and 4800 bauds. This mode is still cheaper for online searching. Average telecommunication cost for a search duration of five minutes will be around Rs. 60 whereas with Dialup data services it will be around Rs. 1200 and telex mode is still costlier.

Vendors

Databases are produced by various organisations, in very few cases the producer of the database provide access to database. It is very common for the database producer to load the database with an online host. The online host provides the computer for storage of database, software to search the database with back-up services to maintain, market and provide documentation for searching the database. They also update the databases periodically. They have developed a powerful computer system to store large volume of information. These online hosts are known as system suppliers of online service or vendors. As on today there are over eight hundred vendors in the world.

Interactive Searching

Search Strategy

The term strategy has been used in different ways in the information retrieval literature. It is commonly referred to as a command put to a search system. Some have referred to as search formulation. Sometimes it is used in the literature to refer to one's action at a particular point in search execution, a decision about what might be the best way to proceed, a methodology to serve an immediate objective. In a broader sense the strategy can be defined as an overall plan for getting the desired results formulated considering the facilities available with the database searched, structure of database and the topic to be searched. The result of the online search depends on the formulation of strategy best suited. It is a skill and can be developed by experience and detailed study of databases.

Preparation of search strategy comprises the following points:

(i) To identify concepts.

(ii) To ascertain index terms, synonyms etc. of these concepts.

(iii) To identify proper databases.

(iv) To study indexing features of the database.

(v) To formulate the query.

Output

The cost structure of database has three cost components viz. (1) connect charges, (2) database use charges or hit charges and *(3)* telecommunication charges. Costs at serial number one and two varies from database to database and also on format of output and option offline or online. For getting the output these cost factors play important role.

(i) Online: Obtaining the output of the search results is the final stage in information retrieval online. Databases offer different formats for outputting the results. The results can be obtained either online or offline. Online results became available to the requestor immediately after the search in other words the results are downloaded to the hard disc, before disconnecting the call. Costwise, getting results online is expensive as the connect charges and telecommunication cost is added till the typing or displaying is in progress.

There is also possibility of loosing the communication link and interrupting the type or display transaction. In this case one has to repeat the type or display command which results increase in search cost. If the number of records are more the time taken for downloading will be more and cost will be also more. In such cases it is advisable to have offline print option.

(ii) Offline: Getting offline output of search results means one has ordered the host computer to print the search results in

a desired format and then the call is disconnected. Here the printing is done after the call is disconnected and then the results are mailed to requestor by air. In this option connect charges and telecommunication charges are levied upto the point of disconnecting the call or logoff. Getting the search results offline is economical. Normally the printouts are received with in ten days time.

As of now India has gained a reputation of having advanced information and communication technology all over the world. India is not behind in adopting new technologies in information handling. Dialog in 1972 and Orbit in 1973 introduced computerised information retrieval on commercial basis. In India INSDOC under NISSAT project arranged a demonstration of online access to the ESA/IRS database from terminals installed in Bombay in November 1976. Encouraged with this successful demonstration, INSDOC submitted a proposal to the Government of India for setting up ESA/IRS terminals in India. However, this proposal could not be implemented. During 1979-80 an experimental project was undertaken by the Information Centre for Aeronautics in NAL Bangalore to access ESA/IRS databases in online mode between Paris-Frascati and offline between Paris-Bangalore: In 1985 NISSAT launched a feasibility study for establishing online information retrieval centres in the country. This was entrusted, to CMC.

Some other institutions also started using ordinary telex machines for information retrieval. Informatics (India) Pvt. Ltd., Bangalore, an Indian party was instrumental in setting up online access centres in several institutions/concerns. Some of them were BHEL, DESIDOC, CFTRI, NCL etc.

NCL established contacts with one of the largest database vendor viz., M/S. DIALOG Information Services, Palo Alto California, USA, for interactive searching of international databases in 1984. The mode of access was telex. One year later similar arrangements were made with M/S. STN International, a subsidiary of Chemical Abstracts Service, Washington, USA. Upto June 1988 this facility was for R&D work of NCL only.

National Centres

Government of India under Department of Scientific and Industrial Research (DSIR) has initiated to set up five online access centres to search computerised databases. These centres are called NISSAT Access Centres for International Data Centres (NACID) and are situated at the following places:

(1) INSDOC, New Delhi
(2) NAL, Bangalore
(3) NCL, Pune
(4) CLRI, Chennai
(5) IACS, Kolkata.

The functions of these centres have been identified as:

(i) To maintain the facility for online access to international data centres.
(ii) To assist the users in formulation of queries and actual conduct of the search.
(iii) To conduct training courses and user orientation programmes in query formulation and search techniques.
(iv) To collect interest profiles from potential users and provide SDI services.
(v) To promote use of online interactive facilities and therefore to promote and communicate relevant publicity materials.
(vi) To recover costs from the users as per the policy laid down for the centre.
(vii) The centre at NCL will cater to the needs of Western Region comprising Gujarat, Madhya Pradesh,

Maharashtra, Dadra and Nagar Haveli, Goa, Daman and Diu.

Experiment at NCL: Online search facility was introduced in NCL from 1984 for inhouse user, with access facility to M/S. Dialog Information Services, USA. The mode of access was telex. With the establishment of NACID Centre, this facility was extended to outside users in 1988. The centre has created the following facilities:

Terminals

Telex Mode

Under this mode the databases are accessed through telex line using the under mentioned equipments.

— Message Communication Terminal (MCT)

— Dot Matrix Printer

The data transmission speed is 50 bauds per second.

Dialup Data Service (PSTN) Telephone Mode

Under this mode telephone channels are used to transmit the data. The speed of transmission varies from 300 bauds per second. The following equipment have been procured for this mode.

— PC/AT with 20MB Hard disc, colour monitor, two serial and two parallel ports

— One dot matrix printer

— One modem (300-1200 bps)

— Telephone line with ISTD facility

— Communication Softwares: *(a)* Procomm, *(b)* Dialog link.

Gateway Packet Switched Services (GPSS) / Packet Assembler / Disassember (PAD)

Videsh Sanchar Nigam Ltd. (VSNL) has extended the facility of data transmission from Pune through PAD in 1989. NCL has acquired this facility to conduct online searches of international databases. The equipment procured for PSTN mode are used for this mode also. The only additional facility created was to obtain a nodal point from VSNL for GPSS access. The speed of transmission is 1200 bauds per second.

Database Vendors

NCL has established contacts with (i) Dialog Information Services, USA; (ii) STN International, USA and *(iii)* Easynet. Over six hundred databases are available for online search through these vendors.

Search Tools

Computerised database producers use different technique of indexing and organising the records. Users are to know these techniques for retrieving the desired record effectively. Datacentres has installed mostly mainframe computers to manage the files using their own softwares. Users have to know the searching facilities provided in these softwares. A number of search aids for online accessing are circulated by the database vendors and database producers. These are known as searching manuals and database chapters. The centre has procured 20 database chapters, 30 searching manuals and 10 thesaurii.

Manpower

Sufficient manpower with proper training and expertise has also been created at the centre.

Cost Effectiveness

In fact, the cost in interactive searching of computerised databases consists of the following components.

(i) *Hit charges:* This is the charge levied on the references selected for a given topic. This varies according to details copied or printed minimum for the record number and maximum for the full details. The cost can be controlled by selecting the proper details/format of output and also the relevant records.

(ii) *Computer connect charge:* This is the charge database vendor levy on the use of their system. It is dependent on the database to be searched and is measured on connect time basis. To economize this cost the search strategy must be well defined, short and properly structured.

(iii) *Telecommunication Charges:* This is the charge levied by the agencies providing telecommunication facilities and is dependent on volume of data transferred or duration of connection. Thus if the system is slow, the searching cost will be higher. Even the computer connect charge will also go up, hence effort should be made to use faster transmission media. First preference should be given to GPSS, there after PSTN and lastly Telex mode.

(iv) *Terms used:* Some database vendors levy charges on the number of index terms used in searching. This can be economized through judicious selection of index terms and structuring of search strategy.

Further the undermentioned points may be adopted to economize the search cost.

(i) To define the search topic precisely.

(ii) To select proper index terms by consulting database chapters and thesaurus.

(iii) To prepare search strategy before logging in and store it in the computer in advance.

(iv) To use special features of databases e.g. use registry number while searching Chemical Abstracts database, which is faster and precise as compared to index terms.

(v) To use faster mode of communication preferably GPSS if available.

Manual vs. Computerised Searching

From the aforesaid discussion it is evident that the computerised search is much faster than the manual search. Cost wise also the manual search appears to be costlier. But the major point of doubt will be in respect of recall ratio many information science experts have opined that the recall is not very high. This may be true in case of generalist approach. But in precise searching e.g.searching through registry numbers for chemicals must be cent per cent or nearer to it. It can be safely concluded that computerised searching is quicker and chapter under the present conditions in the country.

Time

It has been observed that average time taken for a search is highest for medicine (10.3 minutes) and the lowest for Engineering Science (4.71 minutes). Topics in economics has taken longer time (8.7 minutes) nearer to medicine while chemical sciences has taken less time very close to engineering (4.9 minutes). This shows that databases on engineering chemicals sciences are faster in searching as compared to medicine and economics.

3

DIGITAL LIBRARY: ELEMENTS, CONCEPTS AND SCOPE

> "Digital libraries are organizations that provide the resources, including the specialized staff, to select, structure, offer intellectual access to, interpret, distribute, preserve the integrity of, and ensure the persistence over time of collections of digital works so that they are readily and economically available for use by a defined community or set of communities."

The libraries of information era are popularly known as digital or electronic libraries. Here will discuss some salient features of digital libraries in pros and cons.

The idea of easy, finger-tip access to information-what we conceptualize as digital libraries today-began with Vannenar Bush's Memex machine (Bush, 1945) and has continued to evolve with each advance in information technology. With the arrival of computers, the concept centered on large bibliographic databases, the now familiar online retrieval and public access systems that are part of any contemporary library.

When computers were connected into large networks forming the Internet, the concept evolved again, and research turned to creating libraries of digital information that could be accessed by anyone from anywhere in the world. Phrases like "virtual library," "electronic library," "library without walls" and, most recently, "digital library," all have been used interchangeably to describe this broad concept. But what does this phrase mean? What is digital library? And what are the issues and challenges in creating them? Moreover, what are the issues involved in creating a coordinated scheme of digital libraries? It has been suggested that digital libraries will only be viable within such a scheme (Chapman and Kenny, 1996).

Of course, the concept of digital library has multiple senses that one might invoke in various contexts. For example, the concept may refer simply to the notion of collection without reference to organization, intellectual accessibility or service attributes. This extended sense seems to be in play, for example, when we hear the World Wide Web described as a digital library. The concept might also refer to the organization underlying the collection, or even more specifically to the computer-based system in which the collection resides. The latter sense seems to be most operative in the NSF digital library initiative programme. See, for example, C.L. Borgman, et al. *Social Aspects of Digital Libraries*. Digital *libraries* might also be distinguished from digital *archives* to emphasize the nature of the works collected or, as in *Preserving Digital Information: Report of the Task Force on the Archiving of Digital Information*, to stress the preservation function.

One could, of course, revise, refine, and otherwise improve this comprehensive definition. However, it is meant here mainly to suggest that there is a set of attributes that gives coherence to the concept of digital libraries. These attributes include functions of collection, organization, preservation, access and economy. A programme for the development of "federated" digital libraries needs to be defined and measured in terms of the development of these attributes. However, the proposed definition also emphasizes that "digital libraries" need to be defined and measured in relation to the communities they serve. Thus, the DLF programme aims to situate the development of digital libraries in a larger context of service.

MAIN ELEMENTS

1. Digitizing

Digitizing or digitization is representing an object, image, document or a signal (usually an analog signal) by a discrete set of its points or samples. The result is called "digital representation" or, more specifically, a "digital image", for the object, and "digital form", for the signal. McQuail identifies the process of digitalization having immense significance to the computing ideals as it "allows information of all kinds in all formats to be carried with the same efficiency and also intermingled". (2000: 28)

Analog signals are continuously variable, both in the number of possible values of the signal *at* a given time, as well as in the number of points in the signal *in* a given period of time. However, digital signals are discrete in both of those respects, and so a digitization can only ever be an approximation of the signal it represents. A digital signal may be represented by a sequence of integers. Digitization is performed by reading an analog signal A, and, at regular time intervals (sampling frequency), representing the value of A at that point by an integer. Each such reading is called a sample. A series of integers can be transformed back into an analog signal that approximates the original analog signal. Such a transformation is called DA conversion. There are two factors determining how close such an approximation to an analog signal A a digitization D can be, namely the sampling rate and the number of bits used to represent the integers.

The term digitization is often used when diverse forms of information, including text, sound, image and voice, are encoded in a single 0-1 binary code. Digital information exists in only one of two forms -0 or 1- which are called bits (a contraction of 'binary digits'), and the sequences of 0s and 1s that constitute information are called bytes. The term is often used for the scanning of analog sources, such as printed photos or taped videos into computers for editing, but it also can refer to audio (where sampling rate is often measured in kilohertz) and textures map transformation. In this last case, as in normal photos, sampling rate refers to the resolution of the image (often measured in pixel per inch). Digitizing is the primary way of storing images in a form suitable for transmission and computer processing.

Digitizing is making a digital representation of geographical features within a raster image or vector using a geographic information system, i.e, the creation of electronic maps, either from various geographical imagery or by digitizing the traditional paper maps. Since the advent of digital video the term continues to be frequently used, as of 2005, to refer to the process of importing footage into a computer via a FireWire cable. But this is not technically accurate, as the footage is already digital, so it is not really being digitized, but rather encoded into whatever format the non-linear video editing software uses.

"Digitization" is also used to describe the process of populating databases with files or data. While this usage is technically inaccurate, it originates for the previously-proper use of the term to describe the part of the process which involved converting the analog sources (printed pictures, printed brochures, etc.) into the digital representation before uploading to the target database(s). Digitizing is also used in the field of apparel where an image is recreated by artists with the help of embroidery digitizing software tools and saved as embroidery machine code. This machine code is fed into an embroidery machine and embroidered onto apparels. The most supported format is DST file. Digitizing also refers to the process of acquiring precise dimensions from a real world object, such as a car, using a CMM (Computer-Aided Manufacturing Measurement) device. Common digitization methods include optical 3d (laser) scanners as well.

Analog to Digital

Analog signals are continuous electrical signals. Digital signals are non-continuous. Nearly all recorded music has been digitized. About 12 percent of the 500,000+ movies listed on the Internet Movie Database are digitized on DVD.

Processes

The broad use of internet and the increasing popularity of Lean philosophy has also increased the use and meaning of "digitalizing". It is now often used in order to describe the work of improving organizational processes. This will often involve some kind of a Lean process in order to simplify process activities. In many organization this will be followed up with an effort of improving the efficiency in the new "lean and mean" process by digitalizing data and activities. There are no doubt that internet technology have improved many valuechains and also shifted the focus on organizational cooperation into the "battlefield" of value chain cooperation and competition.

Analog Texts to Digital

About 5 percent of texts have been digitized as of 2006. Older print books are being scanned and optical character recognition technologies applied by academic and public libraries, foundations, and private companies like Google. Unpublished text documents on paper which have some enduring historical or research value are being digitized by libraries and archives, though frequently at a much slower rate than for books (see digital libraries). In many cases, archives have replaced microfilming with digitization as a means of preserving and providing access to unique documents.

Implications of Digitalisation

This shift to digitalisation in the contemporary media world has created implications for traditional mass media products, however these "limitations are still very unclear" (McQuial, 2000:

28). The more technology advances, the more converged the realm of mass media will become with less need for traditional communication technologies. For example, the Internet has transformed many communication norms, creating more efficiency for not only individuals, businesses also. However, McQuail suggests traditional media have also benefited greatly from new media, allowing more effective and efficient resources available (2000: 28).

Collaborative Digitization Projects

There are many collaborative digitization projects throughout the United States. Two of the earliest projects were the Collaborative Digitization Project in Colorado and NC ECHO - North Carolina Exploring Cultural Heritage Online, based at the State Library of North Carolina.

These projects establish and publish best practices for digitization and work with regional partners to digitize cultural heritage materials. Additional criteria for best practice have more recently been established in the UK, Australia and the European Union. Wisconsin Heritage Online is a collaborative digitization project modeled after the Colorado Collaborative Digitization Project. Wisconsin uses a wiki to build and distribute collaborative documentation. Georgia's collaborative digitization programme, the Digital Library of Georgia, presents a seamless virtual library on the state's history and life, including more than a hundred digital collections from 60 institutions and 100 agencies of government. The Digital Library of Georgia is a GALILEO initiative based at the University of Georgia Libraries.

In South-Asia Nanakshahi trust is digitizing manuscripts of Gurmukhi Script.

Library Preservation

Digital preservation at its most basic definition is a series of activities aimed towards ensuring access to digital materials over time. Digitization is a means of creating digital surrogates of analog materials such as books, newspapers, microfilm, and videotapes. Digitization can provide a means of preserving the content of the materials by creating an accessible facsimile of the object in order to put less strain on already fragile originals.

The prevalent Brittle Books issue facing libraries across the world is looking towards a digital solution in long term preservation. For centuries, books were printed on wood-pulp paper, which turns acidic over the period of its decay. As the paper ages, it deteriorates to a point of being completely unusable. In theory, if these widely circulated titles are not treated with de-acidification processes, the materials upon those acid pages will be lost forever. As technology evolves, it is increasingly becoming a preferred method of preserving these materials - mainly because it can provide easier access points and significantly reduced amounts of physical storage space.

Google, Inc. has taken steps towards attempting to digitize every title with "Google Book Search". While some academic libraries are in contract with the service, issues of copyright law violations threaten to derail the project. However, it does provide - at the very least - an online consortium for libraries to exchange information and for researchers to search for titles as well as review the materials.

Fiction

Works of science-fiction often include the term digitize as the act of transforming people into digital signals and sending them into a computer. When that happens, the people disappear from the real world and appear in a computer world (as featured in the cult film *Tron*, the animated series *Code: Lyoko*, or the late 1980s live-action series *Captain Power and the Soldiers of the Future*). In the video game Beyond Good and Evil the protagonists holographic friend digitizes the players inventory items.

2. Book Scanning

In fact, Book scanning is the process of converting physical books into digital images or electronic books (e-books) via image scanning. This is a much less time-intensive method than re-typing all of the text; before scanning became feasible, re-typing was generally the only option. Once a book has been digitally scanned, the images are available for rapid distribution, reproduction, and on-screen reading. Such book images are commonly stored in a DjVu, Portable Document Format (PDF), or Tagged Image File Format (TIFF). One can reap additional benefits by using optical character recognition (OCR) to convert images of book pages into a machine-processable encoding of the book's text, dramatically reducing the storage needed for the book and allowing the text to be reformatted, searched, or used as input for text processing applications such as natural language processing.

Commercial Book Scanners

Commercial book scanners are not like normal scanners; these book scanners are usually a high quality digital camera with light sources on either side of the camera mounted on some sort of frame to provide easy access for a person or machine to flip the pages of the book. Some models involve V-shaped book cradles, which provide support for book spines and also center book position automatically.

The advantage of this type of scanner is that it is very fast, compared to the productivity of overhead scanners. Compared with traditional overhead scanners whose prices normally start from US$10,000 upwards, this type of digital camera-based book scanner is much more cost-effective.

Projects like Project Gutenberg, Google Book Search, and the Open Content Alliance scan books on a large scale. One of the main challenges to this is the sheer volume of books that must be scanned, expected to be in the tens of millions. All of these must be scanned and then made searchable online for the public to use as a universal library. Currently, there are 3 main ways that large organizations are relying on: outsourcing, scanning in house using commercial book scanners, and scanning in house using robotic scanning solutions. As for outsourcing, books are often shipped to be scanned by low-cost sources such as India or China. Alternatively, due to convenience, safety and technology improvement, many organizations choose to scan in-house by using either overhead scanners which are time-consuming, or digital camera-based scanning solutions which are substantially faster, and is a method employed by Internet Archive as well as Google.

Traditional methods have included cutting off the book's spine and scanning the pages in a scanner with automatic page-feeding capability, with rebinding of the loose pages occurring afterwards. Once the page is scanned, the data is either entered manually or via OCR, another major cost of the book scanning projects. Due to copyright issues, most scanned books are those that are out of copyright; however, Google Book Search is known to scan books still protected under copyright unless the publisher specifically excludes them.

Destructive Scanning

For book scanning on a low budget, the least expensive method to scan a book or magazine is to cut off the binding. This converts the book or magazine into a sheaf of looseleaf papers, which can then be loaded into a standard automatic document feeder and scanned using inexpensive and common scanning technology. While this is definitely not a desirable solution for very old and uncommon books, it is a useful tool for book and magazine scanning where the book is not an expensive collector's item and replacement of the scanned content is easy. There are two technical difficulties with this process, first with the cutting and second with the scanning.

Cutting: The proper method of cutting a stack of 500 to 1000 pages in one pass is accomplished with a guillotine paper cutter. This is a large steel table with a paper vise that screws down onto the stack and firmly secures it before cutting. The cut is accomplished with a large sharpened steel blade which moves straight down and cuts the entire length of each sheet all at once. A lever on the blade permits several hundred pounds of force to be applied to the blade for a quick one-pass cut. A clean cut through a thick stack of paper cannot be done with a traditional inexpensive sickle-shaped hinged paper cutter.

These cutters are only intended for a few sheets, with up to ten sheets being the practical cutting limit. A large stack of paper applies torsional forces on the hinge, pulling the blade away from the cutting edge on the table. The cut becomes more inaccurate as the cut moves away from the hinge, and the force required to hold the blade against the cutting edge increases as the cut moves away from the hinge.

The guillotine cutting process dulls the blade over time and which must be resharpened. Coated paper such as slick magazine paper dulls the blade more rapidly than plain book paper, due to the kaolinite clay coating. Additionally, knifing an entire hardcover book causes excessive wear due to cutting through the hardcover backing. Instead the outer cover is removed and just the internal bound paper stack is cut.

Scanning: Once the paper is liberated from the spine, it can be singly scanned one sheet at a time in a traditional flatbed scanner. However this is a slow and laborious process. It is instead much easier to use an automatic document feeder (ADF) to scan the material. Some types of books can be difficult to scan in an ADF due to the book having a decorative riffled edging or curving in an arc due to a non-flat binding. An ADF is intended to scan pages which are all of uniform shape and size, and this nonuniform sizing can lead to improper scanning. For these books, the riffled edges or curved edge is guillotined off to render the outer edges flat and smooth before the binding is cut.

The coated paper slickness of magazines and bound textbooks can make them difficult for the rollers in an ADF to pick up and guide along the paper path. An ADF which uses a series of rollers and channels to flip sheets over may be subject to many jams and misfeeds. Generally there are fewer problems by using as straight of a paper path as is possible, with few bends and curves. The clay can also rub off the paper over time and coat sticky pickup rollers, making them loosely grip the paper. The ADF rollers may need periodic cleaning to prevent this slipping.

Magazines can pose a bulk-scanning challenge due to small nonuniform sheets of paper in the stack, such as magazine subscription cards and fold out pages. These need to be removed before the bulk scan begins, and are either scanned separately if they include worthwhile content, or are simply left out of the scan process.

Non-Destructive Scanning

In recent years, software driven machines and robots have been developed to scan books without the need of disbinding them in order to preserve both the contents of the document and a digital photo archive of its current state. This recent trend has been due in part to ever improving imaging technologies that allow a high quality digital archive image to be captured with little or no damage to a rare or fragile book in a reasonably short period of time. Some high-end scanning systems employ vacuum and air and static charges to turn pages while imaging is performed automatically, usually from a high resolution camera located over an adjustable v-shaped cradle. Images are then shuttled from the imaging device into various editing suites which can further process the images for either an archival-quality file such as TIFF or JPEG 2000, or a web-friendly output such as JPEG or PDF.

3. Digital Preservation

In fact, Digital preservation is the management of digital information over time. Preservation of digital information is widely considered to require more constant and ongoing attention than preservation of other media. This constant input of effort, time, and money to handle rapid technological and organizational advance is considered the main stumbling block for preserving digital information. Indeed, while we are still able to read our written heritage from several thousand years ago, the digital information created merely a decade ago is in serious danger of being lost, creating a digital Dark Age.

Digital preservation can therefore be seen as the set of processes and activities that ensure continued access to information and all kinds of records, scientific and cultural heritage existing in digital formats. This includes the preservation of materials resulting from digital reformatting, but particularly information that is born-digital and has no analog counterpart. In the language of digital imaging and electronic resources, preservation is no longer just the product of a programme but an ongoing process. In this regard the way digital information is stored is important in ensuring their longevity. The long-term storage of digital information is assisted by the inclusion of preservation metadata. Digital preservation is defined as: long-term, error-free storage of digital information, with means for retrieval and interpretation, for the entire time span the information is required for.

Long-term is defined as "long enough to be concerned with the impacts of changing technologies, including support for new media and data formats, or with a changing user community. Long Term may extend indefinitely". "Retrieval" means obtaining needed digital files from the long-term, error-free digital storage, without possibility of corrupting the continued error-free storage of the digital files. "Interpretation" means that the retrieved digital files, files that, for example, are of texts, charts, images or sounds, are decoded and transformed into usable representations. This is often interpreted as "rendering", i.e. making it available for a human to access. However, in many cases it will mean able to be processed by computational means.

Remarkably, Society's heritage has been presented on many different materials, including stone, vellum, bamboo, silk, paper and etc. Now a large quantity of information exists in digital forms, including emails, blogs, social networking websites, national elections websites, web photo albums, and sites which change their content over time. According to a report by the US Library of Congress, 44 percent of the sites available on the internet in 1998 had vanished one year later. The unique characteristic of digital forms makes it easy to create content and keep it up-to-date, but at the same time brings many difficulties in the preservation of this content. Margaret Hedstrom points out that "digital preservation raises challenges of a fundamentally different nature which are added to the problems of preserving traditional format materials."

Physical Deterioration

The first challenge digital preservation faces is that the media on which digital contents stand are more vulnerable to deterioration and catastrophic loss. While acid paper are prone to deterioration in terms of brittleness and yellowness, the deterioration does not become apparent in at least six decades; and when the deterioration really happens, it happens over decades too. It is also highly possible to retrieve all information without loss *after* deterioration is spotted. The recording media for digital data deteriorate at a much more rapid pace, and once the deterioration starts, in most cases there is already data loss. This characteristic of digital forms leaves a very short time frame for preservation decisions and actions.

Digital Obsolescence

Another challenge, perhaps a more serious and important one, is the problem of long-term access. Digital technology is developing extremely fast, and one retrieval and playback technology can become obsolete in a matter of years. When faster, more capable and cheaper storage and processing devices are developed, the older version gets replaced almost immediately. When a software or decoding technology is abandoned, or a hardware device is no longer in production, records created under the environment of such technologies are at great risk of loss, simply because they are not tangible any more.

This process is known as digital obsolescence. This challenge is exacerbated by the lack of established standards, protocols, and proven methods for preserving digital information. We used to save copies of data on tapes, but media standards for tapes have changed considerably over the last five to ten years, and there is no guarantee that tapes will be readable in the future.

Hedstrom further explained that almost all digital library researches have been focused on "architectures and systems for information organization and retrieval, presentation and visualization, and administration of intellectual property rights" and that "digital preservation remains largely experimental and replete with the risks associated with untested methods". While the rapid advance of technology threats access of digital contents in length, the lack of digitizing standards affects the issue in width.

In 2006, the Online Computer Library Center developed a four-point strategy for the long-term preservation of digital objects that consisted of:

(i) Assessing the risks for loss of content posed by technology variables such as commonly used proprietary file formats and software applications.

(ii) Evaluating the digital content objects to determine what type and degree of format conversion or other preservation actions should be applied.

(iii) Providing access to the content.

(iv) Determining the appropriate metadata needed for each object type and how it is associated with the objects.

Notably, there are several additional strategies that individuals and organizations may use to actively combat the loss of digital information.

Migration

Migration is the transferring of data to newer system environments (Garrett et al., 1996). This may include conversion of resources from one file format to another (e.g., conversion of Microsoft Word to PDF or OpenDocument), from one operating system to another (e.g., Windows to Linux) or from one programming language to another (e.g., C to Java) so the resource remains fully accessible and functional. Resources that are migrated run the risk of losing some type of functionality since newer formats may be incapable of capturing all the functionality of the original format, or the converter itself may be unable to interpret all the nuances of the original format. The latter is often a concern with proprietary data formats. The National Archives Electronic Records Archives and Lockheed Martin are jointly developing a migration system that will preserve any type of document, created on any application or platform, and delivered to the archives on any type of digital media (Reagan, 2006). In the system, files are translated into flexible formats, such as XML; they will therefore be accessible by technologies in the future (Reagan, 2006). Lockheed Martin argues that it would be impossible to develop an emulation system for the National Archives ERA because the volume of records and cost would be prohibitive (Reagan, 2006).

Emulation

Emulation is the replicating of functionality of an obsolete system (Rothenberg, 1998). For example, emulating an Atari 2600 on a Windows system or emulating WordPerfect 1.0 on a Macintosh. Emulators may be built for applications, operating systems, or hardware platforms. Emulation has been a popular strategy for retaining the functionality of old video game systems, such as with the MAME project. The feasibility of emulation as a catch-all solution has been debated in the academic community (Granger, 2000).

Raymond A. Lorie has suggested a Universal Virtual Computer (UVC) could be used to run any software in the future on a yet unknown platform (Lorie, 2001). The UVC strategy uses a combination of emulation and migration. The UVC strategy has not yet been widely adopted by the digital preservation community. Jeff Rothenberg, a major proponent of Emulation for digital preservation in libraries, working in partnership with Koninklijke Bibliotheek and National Archief of the Netherlands, has recently helped launch Dioscuri, a modular emulator that succeeds in running MS-DOS, WordPerfect 5.1, DOS games, and more (Hoeven, 2007).

Refreshing

Refreshing is the transfer of data between two types of the same storage medium so there are no bitrate changes or alteration of data. For example, transferring census data from a gold preservation CD to a new one. This strategy may need to be combined with migration when the software or hardware required to read the data is no longer available or is unable to understand the format of the data. Refreshing will likely always be necessary due to the deterioration of physical media.

Replication

Creating duplicate copies of data on one or more systems is called *replication*. Data that exists as a single copy in only one location is highly vulnerable to software or hardware failure, intentional or accidental alteration, and environmental catastrophes like fire, flooding, etc. Digital data is more likely to survive if it is replicated in several locations. Replicated data may introduce difficulties in refreshing, migration, versioning, and access control since the data is located in multiple places.

Trustworthy Digital Objects

Digital objects that can speak to their own authenticity are called *trustworthy digital objects* (TDOs). TDOs were proposed by Henry M. Gladney to enable digital objects to maintain a record of their change history so future users can know with certainty that the contents of the object are authentic (Gladney, 2004). Other preservation strategies like replication and migration are necessary for the long-term preservation of TDOs.

Metadata Attachment

Metadata is data on a digital file that includes information on creation, access rights, restrictions, preservation history, and rights management. Metadata attached to digital files may be affected by file format obsolescence. ASCII is considered to be the most durable format for metadata because it is widespread, backwards compatible when used with Unicode, and utilizes human-readable characters, not numeric codes. It retains information, but not the structure information it is presented in. For higher functionality, SGML or XML should be used. Both markup languages are stored in ASCII format, but contain tags that denote structure and format.

Sustainability

Digital sustainability encompasses a range of issues and concerns that contribute to the longevity of digital information. Unlike traditional, temporary strategies and more permanent solutions, digital sustainability implies a more active and continuous process. Digital sustainability concentrates less on the solution and technology and more on building an infrastructure and approach that is flexible with an emphasis on interoperability, continued maintenance and continuous development. Digital sustainability incorporates activities in the present that will facilitate access and availability in the future.

Standards

To standardize digital preservation practice and provide a set of recommendations for preservation programme implementation, the Reference Model for an Open Archival Information System (OAIS) was developed.

The reference model (ISO 14721: 2003) includes the following responsibilities that an OAIS archive must abide by:

(i) Negotiate for and accept appropriate information from information Producers.

(ii) Obtain sufficient control of the information provided to the level needed to ensure Long-Term Preservation.

(iii) Determine, either by itself or in conjunction with other parties, which communities should become the Designated Community and, therefore, should be able to understand the information provided.

(iv) Ensure that the information to be preserved is Independently Understandable to the Designated

Community. In other words, the community should be able to understand the information without needing the assistance of the experts who produced the information.

(v) Follow documented policies and procedures which ensure that the information is preserved against all reasonable contingencies, and which enable the information to be disseminated as authenticated copies of the original, or as traceable to the original.

(vi) Make the preserved information available to the Designated Community.

Basically, OAIS is concerned with all technical aspects of a digital object's life cycle: ingest into and storage in a preservation infrastructure, data management, accessibility, and distribution. The model also addresses metadata issues and recommends that five types of metadata be attached to a digital object: reference (identification) information, provenance (including preservation history), context, fixity (authenticity indicators), and representation (formatting, file structure, and what "imparts meaning to an object's bitstream". Prior to Gladney's proposal of TDOs was the Research Library Group's (RLG) development of "attributes and responsibilities" that denote the practices of a "Trusted Digital Repository" (TDR).

The seven attributes of a TDR are: "compliance with the Reference Model for an Open Archival Information System (OAIS), Administrative responsibility, Organizational viability, Financial sustainability, Technological and procedural suitability, System security, Procedural accountability." Among RLG's attributes and responsibilities were recommendations calling for the collaborative development of digital repository certifications, models for cooperative networks, and sharing of research and information on digital preservation with regards to intellectual property rights.

Digital Sound Preservation Standards

In January 2004, the Council on Library and Information Resources (CLIR) hosted a roundtable meeting of audio experts discussing best practices, which culminated in a report delivered March 2006. This report investigated procedures for reformatting sound from analog to digital, summarizing discussions and recommendations for best practices for digital preservation. Participants made a series of 15 recommendations for improving the practice of analog audio transfer for archiving:

1. Develop core competencies in audio preservation engineering. Participants noted with concern that the number of experts qualified to transfer older recordings is shrinking and emphasized the need to find a way to ensure that the technical knowledge of these experts can be passed on.
2. Develop arrangements among smaller institutions that allow for cooperative buying of esoteric materials and supplies.
3. Pursue a research agenda for magnetic-tape problems that focuses on a less destructive solution for hydrolysis than baking, relubrication of acetate tapes, and curing of cupping.
4. Develop guidelines for the use of automated transfer of analog audio to digital preservation copies.
5. Develop a web-based clearinghouse for sharing information on how archives can develop digital preservation transfer programmes.
6. Develop a list of music experts who could be consulted for advice on transfer of specific types of musical content (e.g., determining the proper key so that correct playback speed can be established).

7. Research safe and effective methods for cleaning analog tapes and discs.
8. Collate relevant audio engineering standards from organizations.
9. Develop a reference chart of problematic media issues.
10. Develop a flowchart for identifying the composition of various types of audio discs and tapes.
11. Carry out further research into nondestructive playback of broken audio discs.
12. Investigate the transfer of technology from such fields as chemistry and materials science to various problems in audio preservation.
13. Cooperate to develop a common vocabulary within the field of audio preservation.
14. Establish regional digital audio repositories.
15. Research the life expectancy of various audio formats.

Some examples of digital preservation initiatives are as follows:

(a) DSpace is open source software that is available to anyone who has the World Wide Web. DSpace takes data in multiple formats (text, video, audio, or data), distributes it over the web, indexes the data (for easy retrieval), and preserves the data over time.

(b) The British Library is responsible for several programmes in the area of digital preservation. The National Archives of the United Kingdom have also pioneered various initiatives in the field of digital preservation. Both use the Safety Deposit Box software from Tessella.

(c) PADI is a comprehensive archive of information on the topic of digital preservation from the National Library of Australia.

Large-Scale Digital Preservation Initiatives

It is pertinent to note here that many research libraries and archives have begun or are about to begin Large-Scale digital preservation initiatives (LSDI's). The main players in LSDIs are cultural institutions, commercial companies such as Google and Microsoft, and non-profit groups including the Open Content Alliance (OCA), the Million Book Project (MBP), and HathiTrust. The primary motivation of these groups is to expand access to scholarly resources.

LSDIs: Library Perspective

Approximately 30 cultural entities, including the 12-member Committee on Institutional Cooperation (CIC), have signed digitization agreements with either Google or Microsoft. Several of these cultural entities are participating in the Open Content Alliance (OCA) and the Million Book Project (MBP). Some libraries are involved in only one initiative and others have diversified their digitization strategies through participation in multiple initiatives.

The three main reasons for library participation in LSDIs are: Access, Preservation and Research and Development. It is hoped that digital preservation will ensure that library materials remain accessible for future generations. Libraries have a perpetual responsibility for their materials and a commitment to archive their digital materials. Libraries plan to use digitized copies as backups for works in case they go out of print, deteriorate, or are lost and damaged.

As is obvious from the previous discussion, the first use of the term *digital library* in print may have been in a 1988 report to the Corporation for National Research Initiatives The term *digital libraries* was first popularized by the NSF/DARPA/NASA Digital Libraries Initiative in 1994. The older names electronic library or virtual library are also occasionally used, though *electronic library* nowadays more often refers to portals, often provided by government agencies.

Types of Digital Libraries

The term digital library is diffuse enough to be applied to a wide range of collections and organizations, but, to be considered a digital library, an online collection of information must be managed by and made accessible to a community of users.

Thus, some web sites can be considered digital libraries, but far from all. Many of the best known digital libraries are older than the web including Project Perseus, Project Gutenberg, and ibiblio. Nevertheless, as a result of the development of the internet and its search potential, digital libraries such as the European Library and the Library of Congress are now developing in a Web-based environment. Public, school and college libraries are also able to develop digital download websites, featuring eBooks, audiobooks, music and video.

A distinction is often made between content that was created in a digital format, known as born-digital, and information that has been converted from a physical medium, e.g., paper, by digitizing. The term *hybrid library* is sometimes used for libraries that have both physical collections and digital collections. For example, American Memory is a digital library within the Library of Congress. Some important digital libraries also serve as long term archives, for example, the ePrint arXiv, and the Internet Archive.

Digital Archives

Archives differ from libraries in several ways. Traditionally, archives were defined as:

1. Containing primary sources of information (typically letters and papers directly produced by an individual or organization) rather than the secondary sources found in a library (books, etc);

2. Having their contents organized in groups rather than individual items;
3. Having unique contents.

The technology used to create digital libraries has been even more revolutionary for archives since it breaks down the second and third of these general rules. The Oxford Text Archive is generally considered to be the oldest digital archive of academic physical primary source materials.

Academic Repositories

Many academic libraries are actively involved in building institutional repositories of the institution's books, papers, theses, and other works which can be digitized or were 'born digital'. Many of these repositories are made available to the general public with few restrictions, in accordance with the goals of open access, in contrast to the publication of research in commercial journals, where the publishers often limit access rights. Institutional, truly free, and corporate repositories are sometimes referred to as digital libraries.

Digital Preservation

Project Gutenberg, Google Book Search, Windows Live Search Books, Internet Archive, Cornell University, The Library of Congress World Digital Library, The Digital Library at the University of Michigan, and Carnegie Mellon University's Million Book Project are considered leaders in the field of digital library creation and management.

Large scale digitization projects are underway at Google, the Million Book Project, MSN, and Yahoo!. With continued improvements in book handling and presentation technologies such as optical character recognition and ebooks, and development of alternative depositories and business models, digital libraries are rapidly growing in popularity as demonstrated by Google,

Yahoo!, and MSN's efforts. Just as libraries have ventured into audio and video collections, so have digital libraries such as the Internet Archive.

Searching

Most digital libraries provide a search interface which allows resources to be found. These resources are typically deep web (or invisible web) resources since they frequently cannot be located by search engine crawlers. Some digital libraries create special pages or sitemaps to allow search engines to find all their resources. Digital libraries frequently use the Open Archives Initiative Protocol for Metadata Harvesting (OAI-PMH) to expose their metadata to other digital libraries, and search engines like Google Scholar, Google, Yahoo! and Scirus can also use OAI-PMH to find these deep web resources. There are two general strategies for searching a federation of digital libraries:

(i) distributed searching, and

(ii) searching previously harvested metadata.

Distributed searching typically involves a client sending multiple search requests in parallel to a number of servers in the federation. The results are gathered, duplicates are eliminated or clustered, and the remaining items are sorted and presented back to the client. Protocols like Z39.50 are frequently used in distributed searching. A benefit to this approach is that the resource-intensive tasks of indexing and storage are left to the respective servers in the federation. A drawback to this approach is that the search mechanism is limited by the different indexing and ranking capabilities of each database, making it difficult to assemble a combined result consisting of the most relevant found items. Searching over previously harvested metadata involves searching a locally stored index of information that has previously been collected from the libraries in the federation. When a search is performed, the search mechanism does not need to make connections with the digital libraries it is searching — it already has a local representation of the information. This approach requires the creation of an indexing and harvesting mechanism which operates regularly, connecting to all the digital libraries and querying the whole collection in order to discover new and updated resources. OAI-PMH is frequently used by digital libraries for allowing metadata to be harvested. A benefit to this approach is that the search mechanism has full control over indexing and ranking algorithms, possibly allowing more consistent results. A drawback is that harvesting and indexing systems are more resource-intensive and therefore expensive.

Frameworks

A digital library can be built around specific repository software. The best known examples of this are DSpace, Eprints, Fedora, dLibra(Poland), and Greenstone Digital Library Software. The Reference Model for an Open Archival Information System (OAIS) provides a framework to address Digital preservation. Other formal frameworks include the DELOS Reference Model(Agosti, et al., 2006) and the Streams, Structures, Spaces, Scenarios, Societies (5S) formal framework (Gonçalves, Fox, Watson, & Kipp, 2004)

Merits

In fact, the advantages of digital libraries as a means of easily and rapidly accessing books, archives and images of various types are now widely recognized by commercial interests and public bodies alike. Traditional libraries are limited by storage space; digital libraries have the potential to store much more information, simply because digital information requires very little physical space to contain it. As such, the cost of maintaining a digital library is much lower than that of a traditional library. A traditional library must spend large sums of money paying for staff, book maintenance, rent, and additional books. Digital libraries do away with these fees. Both types of library require cataloguing input to allow users to locate and retrieve material. Digital libraries may be more willing to adopt innovations in technology providing users with improvements in electronic and audio book technology as well as presenting new forms of communication such as wikis and blogs; convetional libraries may consider that providing online access to their OPAC catalogue is sufficient. An important advantage to digital conversion is increased accessibility to users.

There in also availability to individuals who may not be traditional patrons of a library, due to geographic location or organizational affiliation.

1. *Round the clock availability.* A major advantage of digital libraries is that people can gain access to the information at any time, night or day.
2. *No physical boundary.* The user of a digital library need not to go to the library physically; people from all over the world can gain access to the same information, as long as an Internet connection is available.
3. *Multiple access.* The same resources can be used simultaneously by a number of institutions and patrons
4. *Information retrieval.* The user is able to use any search term (word, phrase, title, name, subject) to search the entire collection. Digital libraries can provide very user-friendly interfaces, giving clickable access to its resources.
5. *Added value.* Certain characteristics of objects, primarily the quality of images, may be improved. Digitization can enhance legibility and remove visible flaws such as stains and discoloration.
6. *Preservation and conservation.* Digitization is not a long-term preservation solution for physical collections, but does succeed in providing access copies for materials that would otherwise fall to degradation from repeated

use. Digitized collections and born-digital objects pose many preservation and conservation concerns that analog materials do not. Please see the following "Problems" section of this page for examples.

7. *Space.* Whereas traditional libraries are limited by storage space, digital libraries have the potential to store much more information, simply because digital information requires very little physical space to contain them and media storage technologies are more affordable than ever before.

Main Hurdles

Digital Preservation

The work needed to ensure that digital content is maintained and accessible into the future is beginning to be addressed: see digital preservation. Technological standards change over time and forward migration must be a constant consideration of every library. Migration is a means of transferring an unstable digital object to another more stable format, operating system, or programming language. Migration allows the ability to retrieve and display digital objects that are in danger of becoming extinct.

This is a rather successful short-term solution for the problem of aging and obsolete digital formats, but with the ever-changing nature of computer technologies, migration becomes this never-ending race to transfer digital objects to new and more stable formats. Migration is also flawed in the sense that when the digital files are being transferred, the new platform may not be able to capture the full integrity of the original object.

There are countless artifacts sitting in libraries all over the world that are essentially useless because the technology required to access the source is obsolete. In addition to obsolescence, there are rising costs that result from continually replacing the older technologies. This issue can dominate preservation policy and may put more focus on instant user access in place of physical preservation.

Copyright and Licensing

It is remarkable that, some people have criticized that digital libraries are hampered by copyright law, because works cannot be shared over different periods of time in the manner of a traditional library. The republication of material on the Web by libraries may require permission from rights holders, and there is a conflict of interest between them and publishers who may wish to create Wenb versions of their content for commercial purposes. There is a dilution of responsibility that occurs as a result of the spread-out nature of digital resources.

Complex intellectual property matters may become involved since digital material isn't always owned by a library. The content is, in many cases, public domain or self-generated content only. Some digital libraries, such as Project Gutenberg, work to digitize out-of-copyright works and make them freely available to the public. An estimate of the number of distinct books still existent in library catalogues from 2000BC to 1960, has been made. Other digital libraries accommodate copyright concerns by licensing content and distributing it on a commercial basis, which allows for better management of the content's reproduction and the payment (if required) of royalties.

The Fair Use Provisions (17 USC § 107) under copyright law provide specific guidelines under which circumstances libraries are allowed to copy digital resources. Four factors that constitute fair use are purpose of use, nature of the work, market impact, and amount or substantiality used.

SCOPE

It is remarkably that at the kickoff meeting of the DLib Working Group on Digital Library Metrics (WG), held January 7-8, 1998, at Stanford University, some discussion was held as to what did we mean by the term "digital library". We concluded that it would be valuable for our own deliberations to document a common understanding of the term, but agreed that such an understanding could only be for the purposes of our deliberations, i.e. we could not and would not aim for a general consensus. This document is intended for that purpose, and this draft is intended to start the discussions. The term "Digital Library" has a variety of potential meanings, ranging from a digitized collection of material that one might find in a traditional library through to the collection of all digital information along with the services that make that information useful to all possible users. As the WG discussed possible scenarios and challenge problems to drive our discussion of metrics, we found the need to come to at least a loose agreement on the scope of the digital library. This document is intended to serve that purpose. Much of the question about the scope of the term is how broad a view should be taken of the digital library.

Does it encompass all of information management or is a more tightly constrained view appropriate? In this document, and for the purposes of the deliberations of the WG, we choose to take a very broad view. This is driven by the recognition that to do otherwise would require setting boundaries that are fairly artificial. The structure of this document is as follows. In the first section, a brief definition of the term "digital library" is given, as a set of characteristics. The remainder of the document elaborates each of those characteristics. At the kickoff meeting of the WG (held January 7-8, 1998 at Stanford University), the following definition was proposed: The Digital Library is:

1. Via electronic/digital means.
2. Available directly or indirectly
3. The collection of services

4. And the collection of information objects
5. That support users in dealing with information objects
6. And the organization and presentation of those objects

Collection of Services & Information Objects

A digital library is much more than just the collection of material in its repositories. It provides a variety of services to all of its users (both humans and machines, and producers, managers, and consumers of information). Thus we start our definition with the notion of the collection of services that the digital library represents.

There are a large and varied set of such services, including services to support management of collections, services to provide replicated and reliable storage, services to aid in query formulation and execution, services to assist in name resolution and location, etc. The basis for a digital library, however, must be the information objects that provide the content. A basic characteristic of the digital library is that the information objects are found in collections with associated management and support functions. The types of information objects vary from traditional "documents" through to live objects or dynamic query results.

Supporting Users Deal with Information Objects

The goal of the digital library is to assist users by satisfying their needs and requirements for management, access, storage, and manipulation of the variety of information stored in the collection of material that represents the "holdings" of the library. Users may be humans or they may be automated processes acting on behalf of or in support of human needs. Users also vary and include those who are "end" users (those not involved in the management and operation of the library but rather are the customers), library operators, and information "producers" who want their material available through the library.

The key to effective collections management is to implement simple structural organizations and be able to present those organizations in a way that library users find useful and can understand easily. In traditional libraries, books are primarily stored by subject, title, author, and date, and accessed by following signs to the appropriate floor, room, bookcase, shelf, and spine-labeled book. The size and relative celebration of each portion of the collection gives patrons information about the collection and can reveal the library's collection management objectives as well. A library is created to serve a community of users. Users who participate in the digital library should be aware of its design and be able collectively to refine that design to better serve their own information needs. Therefore, the ongoing human usability of a digital library depends on the clear and unobtrusive exposure of the library's design, its near-term goals, and its overall objectives. Furthermore, digital libraries should continue the ongoing tradition of coupling utility with aesthetics in the organization and presentation of materials.

These information objects may be digital objects or they may be in other media (e.g. paper) but represented in the library via digital means (e.g. metadata). They may be available directly over the network (e.g., using a query service of the library to find and then retrieve electronically the information object) or indirectly (e.g., the result of the query may give instructions on how to obtain the object, but that is done outside the scope of the library itself.)

Electronic/Digital Availability

Although the objects may not even be electronic, and although the objects themselves may not be available directly over the network, the objects must be represented electronically in some manner through, e.g., metadata or catalogs. Otherwise, we would not consider the objects to be part of the *digital* library.

SOME EXAMPLES

World Digital Library

The World Digital Library is a project of the Library of Congress to make available on the Internet, free of charge and in multilingual format, significant primary materials from cultures around the world, including manuscripts, maps, rare books, musical scores, recordings, films, prints, photographs, architectural drawings, and other significant cultural materials. The objectives of the World Digital Library are to promote international and inter-cultural understanding and awareness, provide resources to educators, expand non-English and non-Western content on the Internet, and contribute to scholarly research.

After almost 20 years of absence, the United States re-established its permanent delegation to the United Nations Educational, Scientific and Cultural Organization (UNESCO) in 2003. Dr. James H. Billington, Librarian of Congress, was nominated as a Commissioner of the U.S. National Commission to UNESCO and was invited to give a plenary speech at its first annual conference in June 2005. His speech, titled *A View of the Digital World Library,* described a vision in which the rich collections that "institutions, libraries, and museums have preserved could be given back to the world free of charge and in a new form far more universally accessible than any forms that have preceded it." Google Inc. became the first partner of this public-private partnership and in 2005 donated $3 million to support development of the World Digital Library.

Planning Stage

At the National Commission's 2006 annual conference, Dr. John Van Oudenaren, Senior Advisor for the World Digital Library at the Library of Congress, outlined a project plan for bringing Dr. Billington's vision to fruition. Foremost was the belief that the World Digital Library should engage partners in planning the four main projects areas: technical architecture, selection, governance, and funding. This was achieved in December 2006, when 45 national library directors, library technical directors, and cultural and educational representatives from UNESCO met in Paris to discuss the development of the World Digital Library. The participants formed working groups to address the special challenges of each of the four project areas.

Remarkably, the planning process continues. The working groups met in the first half of 2007 and included professionals in the field of digital libraries – including but not limited to computer science, library and information science, Web development, and fundraising. The working groups presented their findings to the larger WDL group in July 2007. Findings from this planning process were presented at the 34th session of the UNESCO General Conference in October 2007 in Paris, France. In early September 2008 the Organization of American States (OAS) agreed to join with the Library of Congress in developing the World Digital Library. Secretary General José Miguel Insulza signed the "Contributor Agreement" with Librarian of Congress, Dr. James Billington, at an OAS headquarters ceremony.

DELOS

DELOS is a Network of Excellence (NoE) on Digital Libraries partially funded until the end of 2007 by the European Commission Sixth Framework Programme within the Information Society Technologies Programme (IST). As a matter of fact, the activities of DELOS started with the DELOS Working Group (late 1990s) and the DELOS Thematic Network (2001-2003, under the Fifth Framework Program). The main objectives of DELOS are research, whose results are in the public domain, and technology transfer, through cooperation with interested parties.

Vision

That all citizens, anywhere, anytime, should have access to

Internet-connected digital devices to search all of human knowledge, regardless of barriers of time, place, culture or language has been a vision of DELOS since its inception. DELOS believes that, in the near future, networked virtual libraries will enable anyone from their home, school or office to access the knowledge contained in the digital collections created by traditional libraries, museums, archives, universities, governmental agencies, specialised organizations, and individuals around the world. These new libraries not only will offer digital versions of traditional library, museum and archive holdings including text, documents, video, sound and images, but they will also provide powerful new technological capabilities that will enable users to work collaboratively through annotations and sharing of resources, to refine their requests, analyse the results and access collections in other languages.

Mission

DELOS conducts a joint programme of activities aimed at integrating and coordinating the ongoing research efforts of several major European teams working in digital library-related areas. Its main objective and goal is to develop the next generation of digital library technologies by:

- defining unifying and comprehensive theories and frameworks over the life-cycle of digital library information;
- building interoperable multimodal/multilingual services and integrated content management ranging from the personal to the global for the specialist and the general population;
- developing generic Digital Library technology to be incorporated into industrial-strength Digital Library Management Systems (DLMSs), offering advanced functionality through reliable and extensible services;
- networking and structuring European research on digital libraries to consolidate an emerging community;

- supporting an exchange programme of researchers;
- providing a forum where researchers, practitioners, and representatives of the application communities can exchange ideas and experiences;
- promoting cooperation between European and national digital library initiatives;
- improving international cooperation in digital library research areas.

Organization

Research Activities

Digital libraries support the specialized needs of very diverse technologies and applications, from cultural heritage to general science, health, government, and education. The potential exists for digital libraries to become the universal knowledge repositories and communication conduits of the future, a common vehicle through which information in all forms can be accessed, discussed, and enhanced. In order to fulfill their new roles as universal knowledge infrastructures, digital libraries require research in several key areas pointing to the development of:

(i) user-centred system design methodology;

(ii) pro-active systems with functionality that facilitates collaboration, communication, and information creation;

(iii) generic Digital Library Management Systems that provide basic system infrastructures that can be used to implement application specific digital libraries incorporating context-specific services.

Towards this end, DELOS coordinates a Joint Programme of Activities (JPA) of several major European teams working in digital libraries related areas. The objective is to develop dynamic ubiquitous knowledge environments, which will transform research and education at all levels by collecting, organizing and making publicly accessible on-line vast quantities of information. The ultimate goal is to provide access to human knowledge from anywhere and any time and in an efficient and user-friendly fashion. DELOS also aims at disseminating knowledge of digital library technologies to many diverse application domains, by providing access to technological know-how, services, test-beds, and the necessary expertise to facilitate their take-up. The Joint Programme of Activities (JPA) is organized into the following seven clusters of integration and research activities:

- *Information Access and Personalization.* It aims at developing a uniform understanding among researchers concerning available practices in the fields of information access and personalization in digital libraries, by building and promoting a common and comprehensive framework to serve as a reference point and to stimulate research.
- *Digital Library Architecture.* The main objective of this research cluster is the conceptual and experimental evaluation of the impact of peer-to-peer data management, grid computing middleware and service-oriented architectures on a digital library architecture in order to reveal the advantages and disadvantages of either approach.
- *Audio/Visual and Non-traditional Objects.* The objectives of this research cluster are to establish a common ground of knowledge for European researchers about the state of the art, the research directions and important new applications for digital libraries with audio-visual and non-traditional objects, as well as to advance the state of the art in these areas.
- *User Interfaces and Visualization.* It aims at developing methodologies, techniques and tools to enable future digital libraries designers and developers to meet not only the technological, but also the user-oriented requirements in a balanced way.

- *Knowledge Extraction and Semantic Interoperability.* It aims at exploring the potential of new models, algorithms, methodologies and processes in a variety of technical applications, institutional frameworks and cross-sectoral environments, which will lead to the creation of guidelines and recommendations of best practice concerning knowledge extraction and semantic interoperability.
- *Preservation.* It aims at providing the methodological framework and theory for ensuring that digital libraries research addresses preservation issues and digital libraries incorporate preservation elements in their designs.
- *Evaluation.* It aims at developing a comprehensive theoretical framework for digital libraries evaluation, by researching on new methodologies and corresponding toolkits and test-beds in order to enable new evaluations and to ease the application of standard evaluation methods.

Among its cross-cluster activities, DELOS is working on the development of a Digital Library Reference Model aimimg at providing a conceptual framework for the new research field laying at the intersection of the many diverse disciplines involved in digital libraries (data management, information retrieval, document management system, information systems, the web, image processing, artificial intelligence, human-computer interaction, mass-storage systems, etc.), and on a globally integrated prototype implementation of a Digital Library Management System (DelosDLMS), which will serve as a concrete partial implementation of the reference model and will encompass many software components developed by DELOS partners.

Dissemination Activities

In addition to Scientific Workshops dedicated to specific research topics, DELOS is sponsoring an annual conference known as ECDL, the European Conference on Digital Libriaries. ECDL is the major European event focusing on digital libraries and associated technical, practical and social issues. As for education and technology transfer, DELOS organizes Summer Schools on key aspects of digital libraries (e.g. preservation, access to multimedia objects, library studies).

4

Automation and Data Collection Management

Primarily, Digital Collections Selection Criteria are applied by organizations creating a digital library to decide what material to include. A strategy with defined selection priorities for digitization is critical, and should consider both preservation and access.

Main factors to consider are:

1. the value of materials;
2. the condition of materials;
3. use of materials; and
4. material characteristics ensuring a high level of success.

For the Library of Congress, items of national interest were prime candidates both to improve access and reduce wear and tear on the physical copies. In the early discussions about digitization of library materials the selection decisions were often proposed based on a desire for better access to that item's content, and not on the condition or value of the original item. In 2001, Paula De Stefano wrote that a use-based criteria was promising, as it is "fundamental to collection development and is the common thread in all selection decisions". In practice, however, her study showed that most digital projects focused on special collections, which are generally not the most popular items in the overall collection. The persistent risk of disappearing "last copies", and the declines seen in the condition of national treasures, as exemplified by the 2005 Heritage Health Index Report on the State of America's Collections provide the rationale for establishing priorities and balancing access with preservation needs. The transient nature of electronic information can contribute to a phenomenon called "memory loss." This is a result of data extinctions as technologies become obsolete. There is also a drift away from original bibliographic contexts as time passes.

A 1998 Council on Library and Information Sources white paper identified the following comprehensive considerations for selection:

1. assessment of the intellectual and physical nature of the source materials;
2. the number and location of current and potential users;
3. the current and potential nature of use;
4. the format and nature of the proposed digital product and how it will be described, delivered, and archived;
5. how the proposed product relates to other digitization efforts; and
6. projections of costs in relation to benefits.

COLLECTION MANAGEMENT AND ELECTRONIC RESOURCES

In fact, "Access rather than ownership" has become virtually the motto of the library profession. Dougherty and Hughes (1991) refer to the "transition from the physical library to the logical library" and Michalko (1991) stresses that the research library "must move with minimal disruption from a library model directed pirmarily at ownership of materials to one in which access and delivery play a more central role." This message has been presented, in one form or another, by others prominent in the library field. For example, Penniman (1993) argues that libraries must be active, not passive, emphasizing the delivery of information rather than its storage. Line (1993) agrees that libraries should be evaluated in terms of the services they provide rather than the collections they own, and Dowlin (1993), refers to the need to transform the library from a "fortress" to an information "pipeline." Hitchingham (1996) sees the transition as one from the library as place to the library "as many places."

It is obvious that electronic technologies have already had considerable impact. Virtually all libraries, at least in the most-developed countries, are now members of networks that greatly facilitate the location of sources of information and the gaining of access to them. Card catalogs have largely been replaced by online catalogs and these are being expanded through the addition of materials not previously included. The whole idea of what a catalog should be is changing; it is no longer seen as a tool bounded by the collections of a single library but one that reveals the availability of resources in a network of libraries or even one that is essentially a gateway to a universe of information resources in printed, electronic or other forms. Use of terminals or workstations to access databases of various kinds is now routine for many libraries, and most now add electronic resources to their collections in CD-ROM or other forms.

Remarkably, these developments have occurred with surprising speed, suggesting that the changes of the next decade will be more dramatic and rapid than those of the past decade a point made clearly by Govan (1991):

> It is startling to realize that in 1983, as I recently read, no library owned a CD-ROM... When one thinks of the widespread use of them today, one wonders about the future proliferation of other forms of digitized information: intelligent workstations, optical scanners and optical discs, expert systems, artificial intelligence hypertext, broadbands and satellites, and local

area networks (LANs) and other kinds of networks, as well as devices yet unknown ...

That this electronic revolution in libraries has occurred, of course, is due to developments over which the library profession has had little direct control, most obviously the growth of electronic publishing and of networks that facilitate scholarly communication. Of course, some libraries have been much faster than others in turning the technology to their advantage and thus offering innovative services to their users. One that has been at the forefront is the Butler Library at Columbia University. Its Electronic Text Service (ETS), established in the 1980, integrates electronic primary research materials into the library's collections and services.

The ETS includes several thousand texts and hypermedia research tools in many languages (Lowry, 1990,1992). Similar in scape is the Electronic Text Center at the University of Virginia Library, which has also assumed the responsibility for the SGML-tagging of certain texts that lack such encoding (Seaman, 1993). Several other major universities now have centers of the same type. Gaunt (1995) has discussed their organization and functions. Other libraries or consortia have taken the lead in archiving or providing access to electronic journals.

Now, we will highlight some salient features of collection management and electronic resources.

Electronic Publishing and Scholarly Communication

What happens to the library in the future will depend to a very large extent on developments in related sectors, most obviously the publishing industry. One must assume that the proportion of the world's publications issued in some electronic form will increase and, thus, the proportion issued as print on paper will decline. Less clear is the form that the electronic publishing will take.

How much will consist of resources that can be accessed only through networks and how much will actually be distributed, for purchase or lease, as CD-ROM, videotape, videodisk, electronic book or formats yet to be devised? Of course, what happens to the format depends on what occurs in the creative process itself. Electronic publishing is still in a largely "simulation" stage of development in that most authors tend to think in terms of the static printed page and the static illustration. Hypertext and hypermedia capabilities free the author from static representation, allowing publications that are dynamic and interactive.

It seems likely that future authors, whether research scientists or poets, will increasingly exploit the full capabilities of the electronic media (sound, movement, animation, simulation, color, and so on), thus changing the nature of many publications and determining the format in which they are best issued (Lancaster, 1996). The truly dynamic and interactive publication brings with it other important implications, not least of which is the fact that it cannot be printed out on paper.

The subject of electronic publishing cannot be divorced from the broader issues of scholarly research and communication. Scholarly endeavors are being profoundly affected by technology. As Shreeves (1992) points out. "The emergence of machine-readable texts, of computer-based networks, and of all the attendant technological apparatus, has provided the means to alter radically scholarly communication and scholarly method." He was speaking specifically of the humanities, but the observations are also true of the other disciplines, perhaps even more so. The influence of technology on scholarly research extends much further than the obvious effects of word processing capabilities. Scholars now use a variety of networks to access sources needed in their research, to exchange information with colleagues, and to collaborate with them in research and publishing activities. Some more subtle changes are also taking place. The scholarly journal in paper form has not yet been replaced by electronic journals, although more and more journals are beginning to appear only in network-accessible form (Clement, 1994; Woodward, 1995) and electronics obviously offers the potential for more effective dissemination of information—for example, journals tailored to individual interests.

Network resources have also caused a significant increase in informal communication—informal "journals" now exist within electronic mail and computer conferencing facilities. Such resources diminish the role of the conventional printed journal as a vehicle for the dissemination of research results; increasingly it exists solely to satisfy social (publish-or-perish) and archival requirements. One obvious sign of the increasing importance of the informal electronic sources is the fact that they are now frequently cited in the conventional printed journals. The existence of text in electronic form even alters the nature of scholarship. For example, Shreeves (1992 has mentioned how the ability to manipulate text by computer has changed the types of research that can be undertaken and the types of research questions that can be asked. This point has also been made strongly by Gaunt (1990)
:

> The potential research activities using the electronic version of a text are limited only by the interest and ingenuity of the individual researcher. As social science data in machine-readable form is valuable to the researcher for analysis of trends, for hypotheses and conclusions, so too is the literary text in machine-readable form for similar ends, and for particular work perhaps even more valuable. (p. 89)

Further, the changes in scholarship that have occurred so far may be merely cosmetic compared with changes that could take place in the future. Most radical is the possibility that networked scholarly publication could become the direct responsibility of the universities and other research institutions.

Role of the Library

The library profession does seem to be fairly unanimous in the belief that libraries and librarians will continue to have important functions to perform vis-a-vis electronic resources. Indeed, several writers have warned that, unless the library takes a lead in this, its role will be usurped by other bodies—other departments on a campus or other organizations entirely. Here it is apt to quote Johnson (1990a) who has said:

> "Libraries, in their central role as providers and organizers of information, cannot afford to ignore computer files or to approach them in a piecemeal fashion. To do either places the library at risk of becoming less valuable to and less supportive of the academic community. Libraries will no longer be regarded as the focal point for information as more of it slips outside their purview. Researchers will not longer think of the library as the first resort because they will be unable to depend on its catalogs, collections, and directional tools to provide access to the universe of information resources. The library's significance to the administration will diminish as well." (p. 12)

A similar message has been delivered by Alberico (1991):

> If we don't become involved at all levels, there is a very real possibility that resources will shift to other segments of the economy that can deliver the electronic services that academic and post-industrial organizations will need to survive. It is already happening in some places. (p. 154)

Lewis (1988) has also pointed out that users will demand more from the library than they have in the past :

> Students may expect the library to be as powerful and easy to use as electronic teaching tools. Unfortunately, libraries are rarely easy to use. If analysis with new computer tools becomes easier and more productive than library research, students can be expected to use the new tools rather than

> the library. If libraries do not improve their services so that they remain an essential teaching tool, they risk becoming irrelevant to the teaching process. If this is allowed to happen, it is easy to predict a decline in library funding. (p. 293)

The compilers of one influential report seem to deal that it is almost inevitable that the academic library will decline. Martyn et al. (1990) suggest that individual academic departments will provide their own electronic resources and the library will decay into little more than a study hall.

Management and Collection Development

Given that the library *must* continue to take a lead in the exploitation of information sources in electronic form, what exactly does this imply for collection development Obviously, electronic resources, particularly those that can only be accessed when the need for them arises, present a set of problems that have not been encountered by librarians in the past. As Alberico (1991) points out "Collecting' electronic information is more problematic than collecting printed texts. And, as we all know, collecting printed texts is not without its own problems." Welsch (1991) warns that the entire approach and philosophy of collection development must change: "Simply duplicating the collection practices we evolved for print materials in the network environment does not seem responsive to current needs or capabilities." Nevertheless, collection development, whatever form it takes, still requires policies, as Summerhill (1991) has noted: "The advent of networked resources does not eliminate the need for a formal policy governing the acquisition of electronic resources."

Obviously, a challenge is the problem of how to integrate electronic resources with more traditional forms. The need for complete integration seems taken for granted by librarians and library users alike, at least in the scholarly community; as Dougherty and Hughes (1991) report : "Provosts and librarians... Prefer a future in which there is universal access by faculty and students to multiple information sources in all possible media via a single multifunctional workstation."

Ghikas (1989) points out that the future library must be a combination of "actual" and "virtual" materials:

> The twenty-first century collection will, I believe, be an accumulation of information—bearing objects—printed, aural, graphic, digital—housed within the physical library, *and also* indices, abstracts and catalogs through which, using electronic channels, the library user has access to *pre-identified* resources held by other libraries and information providers. The twenty-first century "collection" thus combines the actual and "virtual" collection. The "virtual collection" is an *electronically browsable* collection. In contrast, tomorrow's library, like today's, will go beyond the limits of its own collection—both actual *and* virtual—in response to specific information requests. In this case, neither location nor delivery time an channel will be preidentified. (Page 123)

The integration issue is also dealt with by Welsch (1991):

> "Technology and technological resources need to be integrated as closely as possible with traditional resources within a unified approach to information founded on principles derived from studies of information seeking and use. Users want to be able to identify information through one access point and not through a series of separate catalogs or information utilities with varying search strategies and command structures that complicate as much as they help. Until a search device, a dynamically updated online guide, or satisfactory resource guides are created, we will have to continue to depend on that hypermedia, intelligent (but not artificial), semi-robotic system that is known as a "librarian." (p. 172)

Further an obvious problem in collection development is that of the costs involved in acquisition or access. Haar (1988) has pointed out that reference sources in optical disk form are very popular with library users, yet they tend to be more expensive than their print counterparts. The addition of several optical disk systems might well mean that monograph purchases would have to be further reduced, perhaps drastically, in many libraries. Moreover, one must recognize the fact that different formats actually interact with each other. For example, an index to periodicals in CD-ROM form may increase demand for periodicals in printed form.

It is true, of course, that electronic resources, particularly network-accessible resources, are economical in space. However, the saving in space is unlikely to compensate for cost increases elsewhere. Moreover, while the costs of computer telecommunications technologies have obviously declined dramatically, and are likely to continue to do so, such cost reductions do not apply to all the technologies of concern to libraries. Another consideration is that, in the electronic world, libraries have much less to show for their expenditures.

Some resources are leased rather than owned, and others do not exist within the library at all. The bodies that fund libraries must recognize and accept this fact. It is undeniable that access to electronic resources reduces the funds available to acquire other formats. As Shreeves (1992) indicates: "Taking the cost of electronic information from current resources is not a pleasant prospect, but it may be the only strategy available for many."

It is Govan (1991), however, who has been most forceful in warning of the economic dangers facing the library in a research setting :

> If any transformation of our present intricate system of acquiring materials should come about, it would change drastically both the practices and the structure of academic libraries. The larger point is that the present system is not working economically for those libraries. The combined

> costs of assimilating electronic technology, recent printed materials, and preservation, have eaten deeply into their infrastructures. For all the professed recognition of information as a commodity, legislators and university administrators have offered little relief and much of the new funding seems to have gone to computing services elsewhere on campus. Any prognostication about libraries future would be irresponsible if it did not lay heavy emphasis on their perilous fiscal state today and the economic problems that lie ahead. All that we have discussed carries a large price tag, and the parent institutions must face the question squarely as to the very considerable costs of supporting a contemporary academic library in a world awash with information.

Van Gils (1995) speaking of the Library of the Royal Netherlands Academy of Arts and Sciences (KNAW), is another who has recognized the need for substantial additional funding and for the recovery of costs through sale of services:

> For the library it is a mater of a radically changing situation, both in terms of expenditure as well as receipts. Looking at the budget and the operating turnover of the Library KNAW I come to the conclusion that for the past two years, and also in the next two years, substantial extra budgets are needed in order to keep up at all with the developments in the field of digital information supply. Achieving a leading position in this, which is one of the objective of our organization for the biomedical disciplines, demands even more money. All this together entails an enormous increase of our annual expenditure, roughly estimated at 15% to 20%. We will have to work hard to recover these costs via existing services.

But costs are not the only issues facing the collection development librarian.

Gaunt (1990) identifies other significant problems:

1. Finding out what is available,

2. Evaluating the sources available, and
3. Acquiring and servicing the sources required.

As she explains, electronic resources are not adequately controlled bibliographically, they are not easy to identify, and they are not well reviewed. The problem has also been recognized by Shreeves (1992):

> ... a major obstacle for the selector of electronic texts is the difficulty of defining the available universe. The usual selection tools (reviews in scholarly journals, national bibliographies, publishers' catalogs, etc.) do not cover such resources effectively, nor is there a developed system of publication and distribution. Finding out about electronic texts requires attention to a number of specialized sources of information. (pp 587-588)

The critical problem, of course, is access and what collection development rally means in an electronic environment. Reed-Scott (1989), for example, sees the role of the collection developer as altering dramatically:

> Because electronic texts are fluid and interactive and are changed frequently, it will be difficult to capture information. Building collections will move from a static process of acquiring library resources to a more fluid position of providing access to information. (p. 49)

Creth (1991) claims that the collection development librarian will continue to do many of the things he or she is now doing, at least in the foreseeable future, but will also take on new responsibilities:

> The context for the future library suggests that rather than relinquishing functions that are currently an integral part of university library activities (e.g., selecting and organizing materials, assisting and educating users in allocating information) these will continue, although in different ways, along with new activities that will emerge. (p. 48)

In dealing with electronic sources that are distributed, of course, the collection development role is little different from the situation in the print-on-paper world, even though some of the sources acquired may not really be "owned" by the library. It is in dealing with the remote sources, those that can be accessed only through telecommunications, that the collection development function becomes ambiguous.

Atkinson (1990), for example, raises the important question: "What role does the research library play, if most research consists primarily in the searching and downloading of information from a distant database by a scholar at a personal workstation?" He hopes that libraries will restructure their operations around three basic functions: mediation, primary record definition, and secondary record definition. *Mediation* involves helping users to identify needed information and to download this to locals storage facilities. In a sense, this can be considered as a kind of deferred collection development operation—locating information sources as they are needed rather than trying to predict the needs in advance.

Nevertheless, some prediction will be required, according to Atkinson. The *primary record definition* role he identifies would consist of identifying resources that are likely to be of greatest interest locally and downloading these to a local database. His *secondary record definition* function is the most unconventional; it is and uploading rather than a downloading activity. In essence, the library becomes the publisher and disseminator of scholarly information.

> When a scholar at an institution has written something which is deemed by a select group of peers to be worth communicating broadly to other scholars, that communication should take place by the library's uploading that publication into the library database, thus disseminating it to other libraries, and thereby to other scholars, throughout the nation

> and the world. The ultimate purposes of the academic library is to provide bibliographic support for education and to serve as a basis for communication among scholars—in short to disseminate significant information. In the predominantly paper era, we rely heavily upon commercial publishing for that purpose, but such commercial publishing is merely a means to achieving that ultimate end—and already that particular means is becoming economically prohibitive and technically unnecessary... The library—in conjunction with the computer center and the academic press—must assume directs responsibility for disseminating information among scholars. Providing scholars with the channels through which to communicate, working with scholars to establish the technical and bibliographical standards and procedures for online publication in this fashion—these are responsibilities which should therefore also be assumed by the library in the online era. (Page 357)

The mediation role, in one form or another, is one that seems to be fairly widely accepted. Welsch (1991) describes it as:

> This is where librarians should find their niche: identifying resources regardless of format and encouraging suppliers of network information to make their products readily and easily available. Focusing their future role not on being a warehouse of electronic or printed information, but on becoming an information utility that locates data in diverse sources seems more appropriate.

The view that libraries should build local databases from network resources elsewhere, however, is not one that appears to be widely held. More commonly, the library is seen as more of a switching center, possibly also having such value-added responsibilities as user education.

For example, Britten (1991) has said: "Libraries should not think primarily in terms of collecting information stored on networks, but should instead pursue strategies for teaching users how to locate and retrieve this information." This agrees with several prominent librarians who see the library of the future as primarily a node in a vast information network. Kilgour (1993), for example, believes that a major function of such a library node will be to build local indexes to aid users in accessing remote sources.

Atkinson (1990), on the other hand, claims that the view of the library as a switching center is a shortsighted one:

> What we have perhaps failed to recognize, however, is that the library must also continue to maintain its responsibility for record definition—for collecting, i.e., for moving a carefully selected assembly of graphic utterances from the environment into a library database, and thereby stabilizing that information for future reference. The most serious error the library could make at this time would be to assume that its role in a predominantly online environment will be mainly that of a switching point. That role as switching point belongs not to the librarys side, but rather to the computer center side of information service. The library's function has always been—and will remain regardless of changes in technology—to select, stabilize, protect, and provides access to significant or representative graphic texts.

Atkinson is supported in this by Summerhill (1991):

> Clearly, groups of local users will have an ongoing need for the proximate location of heavily used data. Thus, achieving a balance between local "collections" of heavily used electronic resources and the provision of network access to less frequently used resources should be the goals of the library acquisition process in a networked environment. (p. 184)

A few other writers agree with Atkinson's view that the library in association with other segments of the research community, should become publisher and disseminator of information. Welsch (1991) has said:

> Yet, the concept of individuals and organizations, including libraries, as self-publishers of new information, who would then make it available through networks, is so tantalizing that I am reluctant, despite obstacles, to surrender it. (p. 196)

Alberico (1991) is more specific :

> The "electronic book" of the future is as likely to be a composite as it is to be a single coherent entity. Scholars will compile their own electronic books by gathering separate pieces of information from different parts of the network. Libraries may become publishers simply by using the network to build customized multimedia documents for clients or by providing the technology, training, and facilities to allow clients to build their own composite documents. (pp. 190-191)

To become an effective creator and disseminator of new information composites, the library must be more active than it is now. In the words of Welsch (1991): "Unfortunately, the image that emerges for me when I think of scholarly societies, universities, and libraries and their roles in the creation of information systems of all kinds is, with rare exception, one of passivity."

One specific problem to be faced in the future is how to deal with electronic journals, assuming that these journals are accessible through networks. Stoller (1992) identifies three options:

> In simple terms, those options are: first, to print the journal either directly from the online file or with the intermediate step of a download and manipulation by word processing software; second, to download the online file to an electronic medium, usually a diskette, manipulate the file with word processing software, and provide access through personal computers; third, to maintain the file on a mainframe computer and provide access through a local area network. (p. 659)

Further, he goes on to discuss the pros and cons of each of these options. Unfortunately, he seem to assume that electronic journals will be little more than print on paper displayed electronically. If, as seems likely, completely new forms emerge—e.g. with analog models or other forms of animation—certain options, such as printing out on paper, remove themselves from consideration. The University of Pennsylvania Libraries (1990) concluded, perhaps not surprisingly, that there is no one best method of providing access to electronic resources. All forms of access—remote time-sharing, CD-ROM, and locally mounted files—are needed. Factors influencing the choice for a particular set of data include timeliness, expected volume of use, the probable number of simultaneous users, and whether remote access (from offices, laboratories, classrooms, and so on) is required. One library that has already gone a long way toward the adoption of collection development policies for electronic resources is the Mann Library at Cornell University, as discussed by Demas et al. (1995).

They identify various levels or "tiers" of access, illustrated. Note that some high-demand items may be downloaded from the national network to the campus network while others are merely accessible from the national network on demand (possibly through the aid of "pointers" provided locally).

Archiving and Preservation

As we all know, the preservation of materials is an important facet of collection management. What are the library's responsibilities for preservation in an electronic environment? Summerhill (1991) seems to believe that libraries collectively should strive to preserve almost everything communicated: "Computer conference logs, electronic serials, even archived exchanges of electronic mails transmissions may all be appropriate for a library to acquire and preserve, given sufficient interest on the part of the user community: "

> **Tier 1**
> Delivered over the campus network via the Mann Library Gateway. Anticipated high demand and need for quick response and manipulation time dictate the use of media and software, which will provide very fast response time.
>
> **Tier 2**
> Delivered over the campus network via the Mann Library Gateway. Must be interactively available, but a relatively low number of simultaneous uses is expected and slower retrieval time acceptable. Therefore a slower storage medium, such as optical platter, may be acceptable.
>
> **Tier 3**
> Resources that can be delivered online via the Gateway on demand, but are not continuously available online. Tier 3 resources may be mounted on request for Gateway access or may be used in the library at any time.
>
> **Tier 4**
> Resources that are available in the library only (i.e., not delivered over the campus network) but that are available from many public access workstations within the library over a local area network.
>
> **Tier 5**
> Resources that are available in the library only, at single user stations

Summerhill goes on to defend the position that even "ephemeral" communications need preservation:

> Those who doubt the suitability of personal exchanges of electronic mail might consider what value such materials would be to a historian of the twenty-first or twenty-second century faced with the task of reconstructing the correspondence of an individual (or organization) who ceased writing letters on paper late in the twentieth century. (Page 185)

Notably, very similar claim has been made by Stoller (1992), but not everyone holds such a view. For example, Shreeves (1992), quoting a speaker at a Symposium on Scholarly Communication held at the University of Iowa in 1991, introduces the argument that not all communication among scholars is scholarly communication and that much of what is transmitted by electronic mail or computer conferencing is nothing more than "high level, high-tech cocktail party conversation"; only peer-reviewed communication can be considered scholarly and thus worth preserving.

Brichford and Maher (1995) suggest that the library and archive professions may be to preoccupied with techniques and standards for the preservation of physical media. Preservation should be more a matter of access to information than the survival of any particular storage media. It is the information and the access points that need to be protected and preserved.

They identify three options for ensuring the ongoing accessibility of electronic resources:

(i) Printing onto hard copy once use has tapered off and interactive access is no longer essential.

(ii) Retaining the original storage media, software, and hardware.

(iii) Continual conversion of the data, with appropriate verification, to newly developed hardware and software.

While the last option is preferred, it is obviously the most expensive and could only be justified if the information involved continues to have high value and to be of interest to a large community of users. In the case of the second option, the library would become a cross between a modern information center (embracing the newest technologies) and a museum (preserving the old).

Notably, Graham (1995) is one of the writers who has stressed that libraries must continue to take a major responsibility in the preservation of resources :

> It will be important to establish standards for the number of repository locations necessary to assure long-term existence of specific electronic information and access to it.
>
> Nothing makes clearer that a library is an organization, rather than a building or a collections, than the requirement for institutional commitment if electronic informa-tion is to have more than a fleeting existence.

The policies of several major research libraries regarding electronic journals (Parang and Saunders, 1994a, 1994b) also suggest that these institutions recognize the needs to preserve and archive these resources and not just to provide remote access to them. While Europe appears to favour the idea of a central depository for the preservation and archiving of electronic materials, the U.S. approach is more decentralized, with the responsibility shared among a variety of national, public and university centers (CEU addresses . .. 1996).

Luijendijk (1996) and Nisonger (1996) have both discussed responsibilities in the archiving of electronic journals. The former considers that this could be undertaken by libraries, publishers or vendors; the latter mentions libraries, publishers or cooperatives as alternatives. Participants in the recently completed TULIP Project (Hunter, 1996; TULIP, 1996) have pointed out why the library community, rather than the publishing industry, should take on the task. Costs and problems associated with the archiving of electronic journals by individual research libraries are discussed in some detail by Duranceau et al. (1996). They recommend that their institution, MIT Libraries, should store locally ("archive") only the electronic journals published there. Access to others would be provided by "pointing" to them, perhaps through some other library-maintained system such as CIC-Net.

Neavill and Sheble (1995) provide another useful discussion on several related issues relevant to electronic journals: archiving, preservation, storage, and "authentication of content." The JSTOR project, supported by the Mellon Foundation, is making significant progress in preserving back issues of important journals by creating high quality bit mapped images (DeGennaro, 1997).

Conway (1996) has dramatically highlighted the "dilemma of modern media," which refers to information density versus life expectancy—the more efficient the medium in terms of storage capacity, the shorter its life expectancy.

Resource Sharing

No doubt, technology has already had a profound beneficial effect on resource sharing activities. What form will this take in the future. Few doubt its importance. Dougherty and Hughes (1991) report: "It was also observed that libraries and library services were no longer individual university problems and that a collective approach is now absolutely essential." In a similar vein, Clinie (1994) has pointed out that "Alliances will be increasingly important to libraries in the networked environment."

Summerhill (1991) has elaborated as follows:

> "Striking the delicate balance between local ownership and network access will be added by, if not achieved by, a formal acquisition process that accounts for network access. Librarians must shift the focus of their acquisition policies from the collection of materials by and for an individual library to policies that weigh the merit of acquiring the same resource by consortia of local libraries, regional library cooperatives, and/or state library networks. The funding agencies that back libraries must come to accept this type of cooperative venture. At the same time, vendors of commercial data products must understand the imperative facing libraries to enter cooperative collection development agreements. Accordingly, they must develop fee structures that accommodate such ventures."

The topic is dealt with by Stoller (1992):

> Finally, on the access level, interlibrary loan must be considered as a potential method for ensuring reasonably universal availability of electronic journals. This seems, on its face, to be a preposterous notion. Electronic text, by its nature, does not seem "loanable." But bibliographic control will invariably result in requests by individuals who either do not realize the title they have discovered is a computer file or who harbor the hope that the host library will consider printing out that file's contents on their behalf For libraries that approach local access by printing out the journals, of course, such requests would be easily met. For others, the level of service they are willing to provide over interlibrary loan will need to be determined, much as has been the case with CD-ROM products. In a world where online computer access is still not universally available to students and scholars, such determinations will have important implications for access to a scholarship in a format that is likely to become increasingly common.

Even since 1992, when these remarks were published, the situation has changed considerably and it is probably no longer true that "online computer access is still not universally available to students and scholars," at least in the most developed countries. Moreover, Stoller is making the assumption that future journals will still be "printable." In fact, it seems likely that the electronic journals of the future will incorporate dynamics and hypermedia features that precludes their reproduction on papers. Ra (1990) was more realistic when she pointed out that, while technology at first increased resource sharing, "it will probably make interlibrary loan obsolete within a generation." Of course, resource sharing involves more than interlibrary lending. The major research institutions that are members of the Committee for Institutional Cooperation (CIC) have taken a lead in exploring the possibilities for resource sharing in a network environment (Dannelly, 1995; MacEwan and Geffner, 1996). Cochenour (1996) reports that the CIC-Net Web server, which makes over 800 titles available, is now accessed about 35,000 times each day through the Internet. Cataloging, bibliographic control and the provision of a user-friendly interface are other services provided by the CIC libraries. CICNet does not "archive" all 800 titles (most are accessed by pointing to their location at publisher or other sites) but has established a smaller managed" electronic journal collection (50 titles in 1996) for which "consistent archiving" is provided.

Thus, at present at least, CICNet is more a provider of access than an archiving center. One possible model for resource sharing in a virtual library environment is exemplified in the initiatives of the Virginia Academic Library Consortium (Hurt, 1995), of which a key element is the recognition of several major academic institutions as regional electronic resource centers.

Libraries will participate in building the statewide virtual library in the following way:

> All participating colleges and universities in the state will be encouraged to contribute online materials to the virtual library, either by providing them electronically to the appropriate electronic resource center or by linking their online resources directly to the system. Thus we have a system of networked resources using distributed client-server architecture and exploiting the enormous potential of the Virginia Research Network to link libraries and educational institutions together. Because the information is cooperatively acquired and maintained by the regional resource centers and patrons are assured easy access, libraries will no longer need to duplicate holdings of materials.

Further, Hurt claims that the consortium will provide "a common system of easy-to-understand menus" and a "powerful search mechanism," the objective being an access system that is "seamless."

Another obvious facet of resource sharing is the development of joint licensing agreements that permit consortia of libraries to share responsibilities and costs of providing access to electronic resources (Gosling et al., 1995).

More than a decade ago, Lancaster (1982) stated that :

> Electronic sources, at least those remotely accessible, do not need to be acquired, nor do they need selection. Rather, the selection activity is of a different kind: Librarians select what to access to satisfy a known demand rather than what to purchase in anticipation of future demands.

To a very large extent, he still agrees with this. However, in the last ten years, and particularly in the last two or three, the profession has given much more thought to what collection development and collection management really mean when electronic communication is the focus of attention. As we have seen in this chapter, views range from the librarian as primarily mediator between users and network resources to the librarian as creator and publisher of new information resources. One does not really know what the world will look like even a decade from now. It is possible that the whole system of scholarly communication will be very much different from the situation today. Shreeyes (1992) considers the collection development librarian as primarily a gatekeeper-one who identifies that portion of the universe of information resources that is likely to be of greatest value to a particular user or group of users. Whatever happens to scholarly communication, and whatever happens to the library as an institution, it is clear that gate-keepers of this type will still be needed in the future. Indeed, they will be even more important than they are today.

DATA FROM AUTOMATED SYSTEMS MANAGEMENT

One could make a strong case to support the claim that the major potential benefits of automated systems in libraries are the data they can provide to improve the management of the library's resources (Lancaster, 1983). In other words, the automated system should be seen primarily as a management information or decision support system. Speaking specifically of automated acquisitions systems, Hawks (1986) has said:

> Not the least of the benefits of autmating...is the enhanced ability to monitor processes, to collect, structure analyze, and report critical or useful data previously unavailable or extremely difficult or costly to obtain.

But the Johnson (1991) survey discusses in this study, clearly shows that better management information is not seen as a major objective of automation in academic libraries and that automation is not considered to have had much effect in improving management or decision making. By the same token the vendors of automated systems for libraries do not emphasize this capability and perhaps fail to recognize the true potentials of their own systems in this respect. In 1992, one of the authors sent a letter to the major vendors of automated library systems in North America, requesting information on their "management information" capabilities. Response indicated that vendors tend to see their "management reports" in rather pedestrian terms, providing fairly routine statistical and financial data, of the type common to business systems in general, rather than more sophisticated reports specific to library needs (e.g. to aid in collection development decisions).

Hawks (1986, 1988) provides a useful summary of fairly routine data that can be obtained from present automated systems. She identifies five major types of management reports.

While she is dealing specifically with acquisitions systems, the areas she identifies are applicable, in a broad sense, to automated library systems in general:

1. Fund accounting
2. Vendor performance

3. Collection management
4. Order control
5. Systems management

Notably, only the collection management reports are unique to the library situation (and even these can be considered as merely special forms of inventory control reports); the other types are widely used beyond the library environment. Systems management reports are reports providing data on the system itself—how much it is used, how it is used, where it is used from, and so on. While Hawks includes collection management reports among the types that present systems can produce, the reports that can be routinely generated by commercially available systems today are relatively unsophisticated. The subject of collection management is dealt with in detail in the next chapter. Fund accounting reports (how much money was allocated to a particular fund, how much is already spent how much is committed, how much remains) and order control reports (what items are on order, from where, when the order was placed, and so on) re completely routine today in libraries of all sizes.

They are not unique to the library situation and need not concern us further here. The vendor performance reports are less routine and, indeed, it was very difficult to collect data of these kind in a systematic way prior to the adoption of automated acquisitions systems. A vendor record, displayable on a terminal, from the INNOPAC acquisitions module. Note how the data recorded can be used to generate reports relating to vendor performance— wheat proportion of the items order is delivered within X period of time, what proportion is never delivered at all, what level of discount is provided, and so on. Carried to its logical conclusion, a vendor performance module might be used to select a vendor automatically based on past performance in the supply of publications of a particular type. Such a capability would be especially valuable in the acquisition of materials that are less routine—conference proceedings, certain technical reports, publications in certain languages, publications, from certain countries, and so on.

Pontigo et al. (1992) have described a type of expert system designed to select vendors in this way. The system described has a learning capability: the performance factors associated with each vendor are updated automatically as the system gathers further data on vendor performance. In fact, the system is designed to rank potential vendors by the probability that they will be able to supply a particular item needed. A similar system, known as the Monographic Acquisitions Consultant, was developed at Iowa State University (Zager and Smadi, 1992; Hawks, 1994).

The system was designed to optimize the decision on which vendors to go tc for particular types of monographs. The knowledge base of the system includes both descriptive and evaluative data on each supplier. Descriptive data deal with type of publisher (foreign, university press, publisher of science materials) and relationship with the library (blanket order, approval plan, standing order, on exchange list), while the evaluative data cover aspects of service (delivery time, accuracy, discounts, shipping and handling charges, and so on). The evaluative elements can be weighted and the system can thus assign a composite numerical score to each vendor based on the company's previous performance for the library. As Hawks (1994) describes:

> "In the selection process the vendor with the highest score who can supply a given type of material is recommended. Once a certain number of orders has been sent to that vendor in a given time period, the vendor with the next highest rating will be selected instead, supporting the library's goal of using multiple vendors"

This system and the one developed in Mexico by Pontigo et al. (1992) were implemented as prototypes but have not been used on a full production basis. Hardware problems and the cost involved in updating the knowledge base were mentioned as problems preventing full adoption in Iowa, although it was shown that the system could save a considerable amount of professional time in the actual selection of vendors.

Along the same lines, but somewhat less ambitious, is a system developed at Pennsylvania State University to determine whether or not a particular title is likely to be received through one of the library's many approval plans (Brown, 1993). Criteria incorporated into the knowledge base, and used to determine probability of receipt, are publisher, subject, price, year of publication, and place of publication. Again, while a prototype developed and tested, the system has not been fully implemented. Other expert systems, designed to help library users satisfy their own needs, have also included document orde-ring aids.

Desirable Reports

If the automated systems now in place in libraries appear rather modest in their management information capa-bilities, Chaudhry (1993) has gone to the opposite extreme in his list of management reports *expected* (emphasis ours) from automated systems.

Collection Use Analysis

1. Circulation statistics
   - number of transactions by patron type
   - number of transactions by location
   - number of transactions by type of material
   - number of transactions by call number
2. In library use
   - ability to record in building use by scanning labels of materials being reshelved
   - supply of information on utilization of collection for staff scheduling

3. Photocopy support
   - statistics on volume of photocopying done
   - provision for photocopy statistics for titles
   - information on number of copies made by titles
   - generation of reports of photocopies
4. Circulation history data
   - provision for retention of historical data on title use
   - statistics on the number on times an item (copy or title) has circulated
5. Use exception reports
   - reports on items not circulated in a specified time
   - reports on items circulated for less than a specified number
   - reports on items circulated for more than a specified number
6. Reserve statics
   - number of holds placed and items recalled
   - reserve statistics by user and material type
   - automatic printing of purchase alerts (when holds against a title reach a specified level)

   - statistics on material booking
   - reports by hour, day, week and month
7. Interlibrary loan
   - statistics on requests received and filled
   - statistics on requests sent and material received
   - average turnaround time

- total number of items loaned
- lending/borrowing ratio

Use of Facilities

1. Discussion rooms
   - inventory of availability of meeting rooms
   - use of special seats/carrels
2. Equipment
   - booking and issue frequency statistics by type of equipment: (AV, microforms, etc.)
3. Terminals
   - amount of time terminals are in active use
4. Printers
   - number of records printed online/offline
   - printer use by terminal and/or location
   - printer use statistics by the hour, day, week, etc.

Searching

1. Searching statistics
   - number of searches performed by search type; author, title, subject, series
   - number of searches by terminal, group of terminals library units
2. Response time
   - High, low, and mean response time for each search/ type of search
3. Searches in progress
   - daily high, low and mean number of searches in progress in any one hour
4. Public catalogue use statistics

Collection Development Reports

1. Summary of orders
2. Subject selection lists
3. Selector performance reports
4. Desiderata reports
5. Material notification
6. Reports of order types
7. Subscription lists
8. Standing order reports
9. Aging reports; outstanding orders sand claims
10. Reports on withdrawals and transfers
11. Holdings and new additions: by location, all number, and language and other library-specified formats
12. Gifts and exchange reports

Cataloguing Reports

1. Online records used for cataloguing
2. Records input from other sources
3. Local/original records input
4. Records created/items processed
5. Records created online
6. Catalogue cards, bar coded labeis, spine labels produced
7. Authority subscription activities:
    - source of authority records, number of authority records input and number of records modified

Financial Reports

1. Fund control reports
2. Accounting information
3. Payment information

4. Year end processing
5. Next year projections
6. Currency conversion reports
7. Fine reports
8. Missing/lost books cost

System Transactions

1. Transaction log
    - activity log automatically printed
    - error messages by terminal/system wide
    - help message by terminal/system wide
2. Database statistics
3. Dial-up access statistics
4. Down time statics

Vendor Performance Reports

1. Orders placed and completed
2. Claims sent and responded
3. Delivery time
4. Returns
5. Pricing discrepancies
6. Discount percentages

Staff Productivity Reports

1. Performance reports
2. Personnel action summaries
3. Staff productivity data
4. Quality control reports

[*Source:* Chaudhry (1993)]

Chaudhry's checklist is useful because it is comprehensive

and serves to remind the librarian of data that might be valuable in support of management decisions as well as that could be generated by an automated system. Nevertheless, the list ranges from data of extreme importance of data re relatively trivial, from data that virtually all libraries now collect to data that are very difficult to collect, and includes data that could not be generated routinely as a by product of the operation of automated systems.

AUTOMATED SYSTEMS IN COLLECTION MANAGEMENT

Automated systems can provide data on the use of library collections that are more complete than those available in the preautomation era. Consequently, collection development policies and collection management in general, should now be better than they were in the past. "Better" here implies decisions that are more effective or more cost–effective: buying more of the things that patrons really need, buying fewer that will never be used or used only rarely, buying more items whose cost–per–use will be low. Various aspects of the use of automated systems in collection management have been dealt with in the literature. Perhaps the most complete overview is that of Nutter (1987). Ways in which various electronic databases can be used to yield data of potential value in collection management decisions.

1. Analysis of the Collection

As Nutter (1987) points out, the online catalog, representing what the library now owns, can be used to produce a detailed analysis of the present collection. Tabulations can be produced for such variables as language, country of publication, data of publication, subject and publication type and useful correlations can also be made–for example, between subject and language or subject and data of publication.

Simple but detailed analyses of this type might in themselves suggest strengths and weaknesses in the collection and the data can be used to monitor changes over time. In an academic setting, the analyses of holdings can be compared with "profiles" of the various academic departments or faculties, where these profiles are defined by numbers from the scheme of classification used to organize the collection. A good example of the analysis of the holdings of academic libraries can be found in the work of Kountz (1991), who compared holdings data with data on student course enrollment to measure the extent to which collections match "constituency interests."

2. Comparison with External Databases

Nutter (1987) suggests that one approach to the evaluation of a collection is to compare it with external databases to identify strengths, weaknesses, items that should probably be acquired, and so on. This seems particularly appropriate to the special library situation. For example, a medical library might compare its monograph acquisitions over, say, the last five years with the acquisitions of the National Library of Medicine (NLM) in the same time period, as represented in NLM's monographic database. Comparisons could be made on the basis of class numbers, where the local library makes use of NLM's classification, or subject headings. The ratio of local library acquisitions to NLM acquisitions in various subject areas could be taken as an indicator of areas in which the local library appears strong and areas in which it appears weak. Another type of holdings/database comparison involves the use of databases searched online on behalf of library users. The bibliographic references actually retrieved in such searches presumably reflect the interests of library users, or at least those who make use of the database searching service.

By downloading the references retrieved by all searches performed during a particular period of time, a useful database can be created. Analyses can then be performed on the resulting data. Most obviously, one can produce a list of journals ranked by the number of times they have been retrieved and this may reveal certain titles that should perhaps be added to the collection because they seem to match current community interests rather closely. Again, this type of analysis is likely to be more valuable in the special library than in the general library.

3. Circulation Analysis

Though it has always been possible to perform analyses of circulation records to study use of the collection, at least on a sampling basis, studies of this kind are greatly facilitated when circulation is automated. Records representing all circulations, rather than a sample, can be manipulated by computer programme to produce data on subject distribution of the circulation, to identify the most heavily used titles and (if the data are collected for a sufficiently long period) to measure rate of obsolescence.

The most obvious application of circulation data is to produce analyses of use of the collection by subject according to the various subdivisions of the classification scheme in use in the library. Jain (1965–1969) pointed out that librarians should be less concerned with establishing the absolute use of portions of a collection than with determining "relative" use. What this really means is that one should use circulation data to reveal differences between actual and "expected" behaviour. Suppose, for example, that books on physics make up 12% of a particular collection. Probability alone suggests that physics books should account for 12% of the circulation. If they do, that portion of the collection is behaving exactly as expected. On the other hand, if physics books account for only 8% of the circulation, one can say that the class is "underused" (used less than expected) whereas it would be "overused" if it accounts for, say, 15% of all circulation. An overused class is one in which items are used more than expected (in a probabilistic sense) relative to the proportion of the collection occupied by that class. An underused class is one in which items are used less than expected relative to the proportion of the collection occupied by that class. If data on the library's holdings in various classes are built into an automated circulation system, printouts or displays can be generated to show for each class what proportion of the collection it occupies and what proportion of the circulation it accounts for. The table shows that circulation in 620 and 640 is close to what is expected, while classes 610 and 650 are heavily overused and 630 is heavily underused. An automated circulation system could be used to generate such data in a more useful format; e.g., identify those classes that deviate most from the expected behaviour–those most overused and those most underused.

Notably, assumption is that the most deviant classes are those that need most attention. The circulation data merely highlight the deviant classes; they do not tell the librarian how to deal with them. One could argue that both overused and underused classes may fail to meet user needs. If a class is heavily overused, the implication is that the library lacks the strength in this area to meet the present volume and variety of demands. The more overused a class, the lower the probability that any particular book will be on the shelf when looked for by a user. Moreover, the more overused the class, the less valuable it will be to the browser because of the phenomenon of "shelf bias." Shelfbias refers to the fact that, all other things being equal, the shelves of a library will tend to display books that nobody wants to borrow.

The phenomenon was identified explicitly by Buckland (1972) and Buckland and Hindle (1969), who referred to it as "collection bias." "Shelfbias" seems more descriptive of what is actually taking place. Buckland (1975) expresses the bias in terms of the proportion of the material absent from the shelves at a particular time. Thus, if 80 books out of 240 were absent, the bias would be 33%. A heavily underused class may be just as disturbing as one heavily overused. The class appears not to be of much interest to the community. This may reflect changing interests over time.

On the other hand, it may indicate that the selection of books is just not a good one. Perhaps the library is buying the wrong books (e.g., too technical or too the -oretical) or that it owns too many books that are out–of–date and should be discarded. It is possible that use of the class would increase substantially if it were thoroughly weeded and more attractive, up–to–date items added. Circulation data can bring "problem" classes to the librarians's attention. It is then the librarian's task to look more closely at such classes to decide why they are behaving as they are and what corrective action appears to be necessary.

In fact, the degree of discrepancy between holdings and circulation can be expressed in several ways. The simplest, perhaps, is the "circulation/inventory ratio" (C/I) used by Wenger et al. (1979), which is nothing more than the number of circulations occurring in a class during a particular period of time divided by the number of items in that class. Thus, a class with seven items and twenty circulations receives a C/I ratio of 2.9 (20/7), i.e., approximately 2.9 uses per item per x period of time (usually a year). Dowlin and Magrath (1983) also use this but refer to it as "inventory use ratio." The Public Library Association (PLA), in its output measures for public libraries (Van House et al., 1987), uses the term "turnover rate" for the same measure (i.e., uses per item per year). Following the recommendations of the PLA and of various state library agencies, many public libraries in the United States collect turnover data, although few seem to make intelligent use of them. In fact, the turnover rate for a complete collection is of very little interest (except, perhaps, in comparing the performance of similar libraries). What is of interest is the turnover rate for various parts of the collection. gives turnover rates for different classes of adult nonfiction for a small public library in Illinois.

The turnover rate for adult nonfiction as a whole (1.11) masks the fact that the turnover ranges from a low of .51 (about one half of a use per book per year) for class 800 to 1.84 for class 400. The turnover rate correlates well with relative use. For example, class 400 has high relative use (circulation is almost twice what probability suggests it should be) and the highest turnover and class 800, with the lowest turnover rate, is used at exactly half the level expected (10% of the collection and 5% of the use).

The data from suggest that the classes in most immediate need of attention are 800 and 920 since both are heavily underused. Day and Revill (1995) discuss a variant on turnover rate in which recent acquisitions only are related to circulation. While this makes sense, it would make even more sense to compare circulation with both total holdings and recent acquisitions.

In fact, Nimmer (1980) has used the measure "intensity of circulation" —number of circulations per 100 titles held. Bonn (1974) proposed a simple "use factor" (renamed as "degree of use" by Gillentine et al., 1981), which is the proportion (or percentage) of the circulation accounted for by a class divided by the proportion of the collection occupied by that class. With this type of ratio, as used by Jenks (1976), the higher the greater the overuse. For example, a class accounting for 3.49% of the collection and 4.79% of the circulation receives a score of 137.25 while one that accounts for .36% of the collection but only .16% of the circulation gets a score of 44.44. Metz (1983) refers to this measure as the "proportional use statistic" and Aguilar (1986) as "percentage of expected use." Aguilar derived his use of this measure from Mills (1982).

Trochim et al. (1980) use the *difference* between holdings percentage and collection percentage for each class as an indicator of overuse or underuse. Mills (1982) is critical of this: a difference of 0.2 would apply equally to a subject occupying 0.5% of the collection and getting 0.7% of the use as it would to one occupying 2.5% of the collection and getting 2.7% of use, yet the proportional discrepancy between holdings and use is very much greater for the smaller class. Mostyn (1974) uses the term "supply–demand equality" in referring to the relative use relationship; an overused class is one in which demand exceeds supply and vice versa for an underused class.

Mills (1982) has applied the relative use principle to the problems of collection development in a film library. In a typical film library, films have to be "booked" (i.e., reserved) in advance, so it has an advantage over most other types of library in that failure rates (i.e., "denials" –cases when particular films or films of a certain type are not available to the requester) are easy to identify and record. Mills makes use of this failure rate, as well as a measure of relative use, to make decisions relating to future acquisitions.

The percentage of holdings related to the percentage of bookings gives a percentage of expected use. Thus, art films account for 1% of holdings and 0.88% of bookings, so the percentage of expected use is 88. The denial to bookings ratio brings in further data. A high D/B ratio means that films in this category are unlikely to be available when needed by a user. The worst case us "stories–holidays and seasons," where 74% of the requests for films have to be denied (D/B ratio = 0.74).

On the basis of relative use data (percentage of expected use), the difference between percentage of bookings and percentage of holdings and D/B ratio, Mills is able to make recommendations relating to future acquisitions: some classes need to be strengthened by further purchases, which might be further copies of things already owned ("add prints"), some need to be weeded and some should be strengthened and weeded.

Subject	*Holdings (0%)*	*Bookings (0%)*	*Percentage of expected use*	*Denial to bookings ratio*	*Collection development recommendations*
Art	1.00	0.88	88.00	0.12	
Dance	0.06	0.05	83.33	0.45	Add prints
Drama	0.08	0.05	62.50	0.31	
Music	0.71	0.80	112.67	0.17	
Africa	0.33	0.22	66.66	0.12	
Asia	0.52	0.38	73.07	0.15	
Canada	0.14	0.11	78.57	0.18	
Europe & USSR	0.74	0.68	91.89	0.15	
Latin America	0.65	0.78	120.00	0.23	
Maps & Globes	0.24	0.17	70.83	0.33	Add prints
South Pacific	0.05	0.02	40.00	0.07	
US Geography–General	0.24	0.19	79.16	0.17	
US Geography–National Parks	0.08	0.09	112.50	0.12	
US Geography–States & Regions	0.35	0.18	51.42	0.11	Weed
World Geography–General	0.21	0.16	76.19	0.30	
Guidance	1.99	1.41	70.85	0.27	Weed
Health & Hygiene	0.44	0.27	61.36	0.22	Weed
Human body	0.36	0.27	75.00	0.20	
Nutrition	0.22	0.27	122.72	0.17	
Physical Education	0.12	0.09	75.00	0.40	Add prints
Safety	0.56	0.35	62.50	0.18	Weed
Sex Education	0.08	0.03	37.50	0.07	
Sports	0.14	0.12	85.71	0.14	
Biography	0.12	0.12	100.00	0.24	
US Hist–general	0.34	0.30	88.23	0.22	

US Hist–Discovery & Exploration	0.10	0.09	90.00	0.12	
US Hist–Colonial & Revolutionary Periods	0.51	0.45	88.23	0.12	
US Hist–1732–1900	0.34	0.29	85.29	0.17	
US Hist-1900-Present	0.02	0.01	50.00	0.05	
World History	0.44	0.47	106.81	0.20	
Creative Motivation	0.89	0.73	82.02	0.22	
Foreign Language	0.17	0.26	152.94	0.23	
Library	0.09	0.05	55.55	0.17	
Poetry	0.17	0.12	70.58	0.09	
Reading	0.44	0.30	68.18	0.17	
Speech	0.15	0.10	66.66	0.17	
Stories-Animals	0.81	0.41	50.61	0.18	Weed
Stories–Certoons & Comedies	0.50	0.32	64.00	0.14	Weed
Stories-General	2.01	1.65	82.08	0.22	
Stories-Holidays & Seasons	0.47	0.19	40.42	0.74	Weed &
Study Skills	0.48	0.34	70.83	0.34	add prints
Writing	0.31	0.27	87.09	0.22	Add prints
Arithmetic Operations	0.61	0.47	77.04	0.13	
Geometry	0.12	0.06	50.00	0.09	

Lee and Lockway (1991) also use percentage of expected use to indicate the most deviant classes in the collection, in this case in an academic library. Sample data from their analysis for selected Library of Congress classes. At one extreme, class HV5001, which accounts for 0.0809% of the collection, gets 0.559^{8}% of the use, a use factor (UF) of 6.92 or a PEU (percentage of expected use) of 692. In contrast, class LH earns a UF of only 0.03 and a PEU of 3.

Britten (1990) uses the "80/20" rule as the basis of a study of circulation in an academic library. He found that, while the rule seemed to apply to the complete collection, substantial differences among the LC classes could be observed. For one subclass, 40% of the items are needed to account for 80% of the circulations. At the other extreme is a class in which only 1.5%

of the items account for 80% of the use. He advocates that the classes that deviate most from the 80/20 distribution in a positive way (a higher proportion needed to account for 80% of the use) should be "rewarded" in future collection development and budget allocation. Clearly, this type of comparison of the performance of various categories of books is merely another variant of relative use or the turnover rate.

There are other ways of expressing overuse and underuse of portions of the collection. One is the proportion of items on loan (and, conversely, the proportion that should be on the shelf) at a particular time. A class in which many of the items are in use is a healthy class whereas one from which few items are borrowed is not—little interest exists in this subject in the community, the library is not buying the right books, or the class contains too much that is obsolete. On the other hand, it is not good to have a class in which most books are always absent from the shelves; this would indicate considerable shelf bias and the probability that a user would find particular item on the shelf when needed must be very low. Extremely active classes of this kind need strengthening, at least through the purchase of further copies of the most used items.

The monitoring of collection use by proportions of classes absent from the shelves is not dependent on automation and, in fact, predated automated systems. Nevertheless, such monitoring is much easier when data can be drawn from an automated circulation system. From Payne and Willers (1989), is one example. Note the very wide differences between heavily used classes, in which more than 20% of the items are on loan and little used classes, in which less than 5% are in use. In performing analyses of this kind, items that cannot be borrowed (i.e., reference only) should obviously be excluded.

Automated circulation records can also be used to identify items in collection that are receiving little use and, thus, may be candidates for discarding or retirement to storage. Use can be expressed in several different ways, including the length of time that has elapsed since a book was last borrowed. In fact, "last circulation date" can be used to partition the monograph collection by "levels of popularity," where popularity is expressed in terms of the last circulation date.

It is also possible to use the circulation system to "flag" items that are now used so heavily that additional copies should be purchased or some other steps taken to improve their availability. In fact, several commercially–available systems have an alert feature to identify items for which X patrons have placed "holds."

Popula-rity class	*Measure of popularity*	*Percentage of the collection*
A	Borrowed in the last month	3
B	Borrowed in the last three months but not in last month	10
C	Borrowed in the last year but not in last three months	25
D	Borrowed in last five years but not last year	30
E	Not borrowed in last five years	32

Special Databases Building

Analyses of circulation patterns of the type discussed in the preceding section are based on data that can be drawn from an existing database–that recording which items are borrowed, when and by whom. But it is also possible to build other databases that can be useful in making decisions relating to collection development and management.

One such database would record in–house use of the collection. In the past, it has been notoriously difficult to get good data on in–library use (Rubin, 1986; Lancaster, 1993a). Today, however, portable data collection devices can be used to scan bar codes or OCR labels on books left on tables or in carrels in the library before they are returned to the shelves. This procedure is likely to underestimate the total volume of inhouse use, perhaps rather considerably, because not all uses will involve carrying items to seats in the library and many items may be returned to shelves by users (Lancaster, 1993a). Nevertheless, it should depict the pattern of inhouse use fairly accurately: if the data show that X items are used five times more than Y items, this probably does reflect the relative use of these two sets, even though both counts may be underestimates.

Rapidly escalating costs, coupled with budgets diminishing in purchasing power, have forced many libraries to discontinue subscriptions to some periodicals or other serials. To aid decisions on which serials to discontinue, it may be valuable to build a database of information on the serials that the library now receives. Such a database has been described by Hansen (1986).

The most difficult data to collect, of course, are those on recorded use. If these can not be collected through use of scanning devices, as mentioned earlier, they can be obtained in various ways on a sampling basis.

Although Hansen records binding cost, she does not calculate a total ownership cost, based on estimates of storage and handling costs as well as subscription and binding costs. The data she does record would allow an estimate to be made of cost per use (see Chrzastowski, 1991, for example) for each serial based on subscription cost and binding cost, but use related to an estimate of total ownership cost would be more accurate. In any case, the serials with highest cost per use would be prime candidates for deselection in items of budget reductions, although the other factors(e.g., local availability, relevance to particular departments, ready accessibility through document delivery services) should also be taken into account.

1. Code for most relevant academic department

2. Subscription cost
3. Binding cost
4. Cost of microform alternative
5. Code for availability in electronic form
6. Code for availability from document delivery services
7. Availability in other local libraries
8. Coverage in printed and electronic databases
9. Recorded use

No doubt, the construction of a database of this kind and its updating and maintenance, require an investment on the part of the library. Hansen suggests that the investment is justifiable because the database makes readily available the information needed to make deselection decisions and has value in other applications–e.g., to generate printouts of serials relevant to particular academic departments and to provide data useful to binding operations.

Although the database described by Hansen is designed for use in academia, it could obviously be modified for use by other types of libraries. All of the elements other than department–relatedness are equally relevant to other libraries and alternative data could be substituted as appropriate. For example, a subject category could be used in place of department–relatedness in the case of a public library.

Yet another type of database can be built to record interlibrary loan transactions as described, for example, by Wessling (1989) and Chang (1990). Interlibrary loans initiated online, by staff members or library users, can be recorded automatically and others added manually. A database of this kind may be useful in a number of different ways. For example, it could be used to:

1. Identify requests made by particular constituencies (e.g., academic departments).

2. Identify monographs or journals requested more than X times.
3. Identify subject areas in which many requests are made.
4. Provide data that can be compared with other data, such as those relating to circulation and acquisitions patterns.

Data Comparisons

Decisions relating to the development and management of collections will be most firmly based when they take into account more than circulation data alone–hence the value of the specially constructed databases discussed in the previous section. Data on circulation, in–house use, interlibrary loan and current acquisition patterns can all be useful. For example, one needs to know, for any particular subject area, what the level of current purchasing is and whether use of the class is increasing or decreasing over time.

Another example of complementary data useful in collection development decisions. It shows an actual collection evaluation report, for the period July 1, 1989, to June 30, 1990, from a public library in Illinois. For each of the Dewey classes, the following data are presented: percentage of collection, percentage of circulation, turnover rate, percentage of interlibrary borrowings for the past year and percentage of acquisitions for the past year. Note here some classes that seem still to need corrective action. For example, 300 is underused and as a relatively low turnover rate, but interlibrary loans are strong (proportionally more than circulation) and the current acquisition rate is very high. The low circulation and turnover, coupled with the high rate of interlibrary borrowing, suggest that what is being purchased in this class does not correspond well with the current interests of users. If better fit to user interests, acquisitions in this class might actually be reduced.

The low turnover rate and discrepancy between collection and circulation percentages further suggest that the class needs some thorough weeding. In contrast, 600 is a heavily overused class; that it now accounts for almost 28% of acquisitions indicates that this fact has been recognized and appropriate corrective action taken. The librarian should look at fine circulation data rather than coarse to avoid jumping to the wrong conclusions. The fact that Dewey class 600 is overused does not necessarily mean that the entire class is overused; it may be that only the cookbooks are overused and all other subdivisions are actually underused. Likewise, overuse of Library of Congress class QA may suggest the need for strengthening of the entire mathematics collection when, in fact, it is only the computer science books that are affecting the results.

Of course, automated circulation systems can yield data that are finer than gross use patterns; use of small subclasses or even individual titles can be examined. One example of this type of analysis can be found in Britten and Webster (1992), who analyzed MARC records for titles heavily used within an academic library in an attempt to identify common characteristics that might predict use of future additions to the collection. Common elements examined were subject heading, author, language and imprint date.

Byrd et al. (1982) have described a method for determining strengths and weaknesses in a collection based on the difference in proportions between the subject breakdown of a library's acquisitions and the subject breakdown of the interlibrary loan requests it generates. The theory is that the classes needing greatest attention are those in which the greatest difference exists between volume of materials borrowed and volume of materials purchased. This discrepancy is expressed as a "collection balance indicator" (CBI), a relative percentage, as follows:

$$100 \times \frac{\text{New acquisitions in this class}}{\text{Total acquisitions}} - \frac{\text{Titles borrowed in this class}}{\text{Total titles borrowed}}$$

A positive value on the CBI indicates a subject area relatively strong in terms of current acquisitions while a negative value indicates one relatively weak. This can be illustrated through two simple examples:

$$1.\ 100 \times \frac{100}{400} - \frac{12}{120} = 15 \qquad 2.\ 100 \times \frac{40}{400} - \frac{30}{120} = -15$$

In the first case, 25% of the acquisitions are made in this subject field but only 10% of the titles borrowed fall in this area. The CBI is a high 15. The second case puts the proportions exactly in reverse–10% of acquisitions and 25% of titles borrowed–and the value is a low –15.

Payne and Willers (1989) have shown how circulation data can be related to acquisitions data to measure success in materials selection (expressed, for example, by the proportion of items purchased in subject X that have circulation within period Y). Success may also be related to source of selection–e.g., faculty versus librarian selection in the case of some academic libraries.

Aguilar (1984) performed a monumental study of the relationship between internal circulation and interlibrary loan requests based on about 86,000 interlibrary loan (ILL) transactions and almost two million circulation records from eighteen Illinois libraries. He found support for his hypothesis that a class that is overused (as defined earlier) in a library will be a class in which the library will borrow many items, whereas underused classes tend not to generate large numbers of ILL requests. This support the assumption that it is overused classes rather than underused classes that are most in need of strengthening.

As a result of his research, Aguilar (1986) developed a measure "ratio of borrowings to holdings" (RBH), which is simply:

$$\frac{\%\text{ of borrowings}}{\%\text{ of holdings}}$$

Values greatly in excess of I would indicate a class in which the borrowing rate is very high relative to the holdings of the library. For example, a class that occupies 8% of the collection but accounts for 15% of borrowings would have an RBH of almost 1.9 (15/8). Aguilar uses the RBH data, together with relative use circulation data, to produce a collection development "model." For overused and underused classes the RBH is looked at. Decisions on the future of the class are made on the basis of relative use and RBH data. Nutter (1987) recommends that academic libraries should study interrelations among databases representing holdings, circulation, and patron characteristics. Patron files can be coded by department/discipline to allow comparisons of usage and to study what types of materials are used each department.

Monitoring OPAC Interactions

Another source of information of potential value in collection development is the online catalog and its actual use by library patrons. Possibly useful information can be obtained from several report generation features existing within commercially available system. For example, the INNOPAC system will identify the names of authors most used within a particular time period and the subject terms introduced by users that do not retrieve any items. While the latter will often be symptomatic of errors in user terminology, or search logic, they may occa-sionally indicate gaps in subject coverage in the collection. In theory, interactions between library users and the catalog could be monitored to identify (1) books sought that are not in the collection and (2) books sought and found to be in the collection but not immediately available on the shelves (which could be used to produce an estimate of availability rate). However, this presupposes that users must employ some unambiguous identifier for a book rather than a truncation algorithm that is equivocal.

While all of the analyses discussed so far can based on data obtainable from library catalogs, circulation systems, acquisitions systems or other databases, this will usually require the writing of special programmes for extraction and manipulation since the commercially available systems are not likely to offer the capabilities sought as a standard feature. Features that are present in many existing systems include: (1) ability to record circulation by type of patron, (2) ability to identify the most heavily used classes, (3) ability to identify books for which many "holds" are placed and (4) ability to identify books not borrowed within a particular period of time (Hawks, 1988).

The factors that affect the availability of books owned by a library have been thoroughly discussed by Buckland (1975). The most important are level of demand (popularity), number of copies and length of loan period. It is obvious that the more popular a particular book the less likely it is to be on the shelf at any particular time. "Popularity" is not a nebulous measure in this case, but a very practical one. As mentioned earlier, it can be expressed in terms of a last circulation date. That is, one could say that 10% of the collection circulated at least once in the last month, 25% circulated at least once in the last six months and so on. It seems equally obvious that buying additional copies will improve availability.

But two copies are not twice as good as one copy–sometimes both are on the shelf, sometimes one, sometimes neither–and the addition of further copies may make only a marginal difference to availability. The effect of adding an additional copy varies with the popularity of the item: if a particular book is never used it will always be available and adding a second copy does not change the situation. If a book is off the shelf for one half of the year, one can say its availability rate is 0.5. Adding a second copy will improve availability but will not double it (Leimkuhler, 1966). Buckland (1975) presents data to show the effect of varying numbers of duplicate copies on the availability of books at different levels of popularity.

Less obvious, perhaps, are the effects on availability of the length of the loan period. Suppose that every user of a library returns a book on or near the day on which it is due to be returned. There is, in fact, a strong tendency for this to occur, as reported by Newhouse and Alexander (1972), Buckland (1975), and Goehlert (1979).

Then, reducing the length of the loan period from four weeks greatly increases the probability that any book will be available on the shelf when looked for by a user. In fact, cutting the length of the period in half has roughly the same effect on availability as buying a second copy. The librarian can improve the accessibility of books by buying more copies of popular items, reducing the length of the loan period, or both. In fact, if one wished, it would be possible to identify a desired "satisfaction level" (e.g., 0.8–a user will find a desired item to be on the shelf in eight cases out of ten) and take steps to ensure that this level would apply to every book in the library. Suppose one divided the collection into five levels of popularity on the basis of most recent circulation date. For Level 5 the probability of availability could already be 0.99 and would remain there even if the loan period for this category was extended to ten years.

For Level 4 the probability of availability might already be 0.8 with a loan period of four weeks and no further action us required. Availability for Level 3 items might be increased to 0.8

by reducing the length of the loan period from four weeks to three weeks. To reach 0.8 availability for Level 2, the length of the loan period may need to be reduced to two weeks. This leaves us with Level 1 items–the rather small number of highly popular items in the library. To ensure a probability of availability of 0.8 one might need, say, five copies of each and a loan period of one week.

Notably, Buckland (1975) has published data that show how popularity (level of demand for an item), length of loan period and number of copies affect the probability of availability of books. With a long loan period of ten weeks, the chance that one of the most popular books (class A) will be on the shelf, assuming a single copy, is only .37. This probability can be increased to .66 with two copies and .86 with three. On the other hand, reducing the length of the loan period, without buying further copies, also has a profound effect on the probability of availability. With a one-week loan period, even the most popular items in this hypothetical library have a high probability (.91) of being on the shelf when sought by a user.

As Buckland's data show clearly, reducing the loan period or buying further copies are strategies that have most profound effects on the items in greatest demand. The data in regarded only as illustrative of the interrelationships involved among popularity, duplication rate and length of loan period. The actual probabilities of availability within this model would be determined by the different values accorded to the levels of popularity (e.g., availability values for class A if it were defined as "last circulation date = one month or less" would be different from the values were this class defined as "LCD = two months or less").

Further, Buckland (1975) has reported that a type of "homeostatic" effect may govern book availability. That is, if satisfaction level is pushed up from, say 0.5 to 0.8, use the library may increase substantially because of improved expectations of success among the community. This greatly increased demand, however, increases competition for the library's resources and forces satisfaction level down–perhaps back to 0.5. Automated circulation systems allow one to conceive of a self–regulating library with no fixed loan period. An algorithm incorporated within the system would tell the user how long a particular book could be borrowed at the time of checkout.

The calculation would be made on the basis of the circulation history of the book and the number of copies held, the loan period being calculated to ensure that the desired satisfaction level (say 0.8) will be maintained. The system would probably work with a large but finite number of loan periods–in the range of, say, five to ten. Of course, such a policy might not be popular with users, especially those who find that the several books they borrow on a particular day all have different return dates, but it would definitely make the library more efficient in terms of the probability of materials sought.

A somewhat different approach to the monitoring of collection development practices involves the comparison of a subject profile of what is being acquired with a subject profile of community interests or probable demands. This is most appropriate to the academic world, where it is possible to express the probable interests of a department in terms of the content of its curriculum, which may be converted into class numbers from the bibliographic scheme in use and the probable demand in terms of the size of the department (number of faculty, number of students, number of instructional units). The profile of interest for the various departments can be matched against holdings, current acquisitions, or current circulation. Example of use of such techniques can be found in the work of McGrath, Golden and Jenks. McGrath (1968) showed, for each academic department, the number of circulated books relevant to the departmental profile, the percentage of the total circulation/enrollment ratio. Golden (1974) related the class numbers associated with a course to the number of books owned in these classes and to enrollment the course in an attempt to identify strengths and weaknesses in the collection.

Jenks (1976) compared circulation with the number of students in each department and with the number of books matching the profile of each department. He also ranked departments according to the use each made of that part of the collection matching its interest profile. McGrath (1972) has shown that books matching the profile of institutional interests are much more likely to be borrowed than books not matching the profile, while McGrath et al. (1979) have used a subject classification approach to determine to what extent graduate and undergraduate students borrow books outside their own disciplines. Power and Bell (1978) propose a more elaborate formula that takes into account, for each academic department, the number of faculty members, the number of students at various levels, the holdings matching the departmental profile and circulation.

Evans and Beilby (1983) describe collection evaluation through a sophisticated management information system employed within the libraries of the State University of New York. In one database were stored student enrollment classified by subject field according to the Higher Education General Information Survey (HEGIS) codes. By using OCLC tapes, together with a conversion tape showing equivalencies between the HEGIS codes and Library of Congress class numbers, it was possible to relate the acquisitions data of a library to the enrollment.

Thus, for each HEGIS code (e.g., 1103, German language), the system would generate a printout showing the number of titles acquired by the library, the percentage of the total acquisitions that this represents, the number of student credit hours and the percentage of the total credit hours that this represents. Subject areas in which strong (or weak) relationships exist between student credit hours and acquisitions patterns can thus be identified and any necessary corrections made. More recently, Kountz (1991) has performed similar analyses. Since student credit hours or credit units in various disciplines are reported to the U.S. Department of Education in the form of HEGIS or, now, IPEDS (Integrated Postsecondary Education Data System) codes and these codes can be converted into Library of Congress or Dewey Decimal class numbers, a profile of "constituency interests" can be matched against collection, acquisition or circulation data. Kountz uses titles per unit of student credit in the various subjects as a measure of the degree to which the collection matches interests.

Further, similar analyses may also be possible in the special library environment. For example, Spaulding and Stanton (1976) and Kennedy (1983) describe the use of the Dewey classification as an aid to book selection in an industrial library network. A selection profile for each member library is constructed, using DDC numbers plus verbal descriptions. Circulation data were used in the building of the profiles. Computer–generated reports allow a manager to determine to what extent materials purchased in a particular time period match a library's profile. While such analyses are not completely dependent on automated systems, it is obvious that they become more practical when the needed can be extracted from databases representing holdings, circulation or current acquisitions.

Notably, significant collection management problem in the academic world is that associated with the equitable distribution of the materials budget over the interest of the various departments: how much should be spent on the acquisition of chemistry materials, how much on history, how much on education and so on? The types of analyses discussed in the previous section can be useful in suggesting criteria for such allocation–e.g., dollars allocated in proportion to student credit units. An allocation formula may be more easily justified if it takes into account a number of different criteria. Again, the development of allocation formulae is not dependent on automation.

Nevertheless, many of the needed to develop a formula may be available from various databases and it is much easier to develop a multi–component formula when the component data can be manipulated by computer. Sample data that have been considered for use as components in a materials allocation formula for a large university in the United States. While some justification can be made for any and all of these components, a formula that takes into account so many components may be too complex to apply in practice.

The major problem involved is that of getting agreement on how much weight each components should receive in the calculation of the allocation. The list of possible components is a long one, but it is by no means complete. In general, it is based more on inputs to a department than on outputs. While instructional output can be considered to be reflected in number of students graduating, research output (e.g., in publications produced) are not considered at all.

For each department:

Size of faculty (in full time equivalents–FTE)
Percentage of total university faculty
Master degrees awarded
Percentage of total masters degrees awarded
Doctoral degrees awarded
Percentage of total doctoral degrees awarded
Instructional units
Percentage of total instructional units
Department budget

Percentage of total university budget
Grants and contracts received
Percentage of total grants and contracts
Items borrowed from the library
Percentage of total library circulation
Size of departmental collection (in titles)
Percentage of total library collection
Average cost of a monograph in this subject area
Average cost of a serial subscription in this subject area

Here it is pertinent to note that Brownson (1991) discusses the limitations of allocation formulae of the type that have been used in the past. He proposes a somewhat different approach based primarily on:

(1) the collection strength desired in a particular subject,
(2) an estimate of the present strength in that subject,
(3) the number if items owned in that class,
(4) the circulation in that class and
(5) extent of faculty research in the subject as reflected in number of research projects.

Ottensmann and Gleeson (1993) and Gleeson and Ottensmann (1993) have described an approach to the development of a budget allocation formula for a public library, based on data derived from a computerized circulation system. The objective is to allocate the budget in such a way as to optimize circulation "within the constraints of other objective established by librarians."

Various investigators have attempted to apply expert system techniques to the selection of materials for library collections. Rade et al. (1987) have described an expert system approach to the selection of journals. While their objectives were somewhat different the decision on whether or not a journal should be included in the MEDLARS database–the criteria built into their system (type of publisher, language, type of article, type of author, publication standards) would be among those relevant to a knowledge base designed to aid a librarian in journal selection decisions.

Meador and Cline (1992) describe a workstation designed to make readily accessible all of the information that a librarian might need in selection decisions–collection development guidelines, holdings and circulation data, financial data and so on. While not an expert system per se, this approach can be considered as a first step toward the development of such a system. Sowell (1989) describes a rudimentary expert system to aid in monograph selection, but he deals only in a very narrow subject area and the prototype developed was tested with very few cases. This study has dealt with computer–based systems as sources of information or assistance in collection development and management. However, it relates primarily to collections in print–on–paper form.

EVALUATION OF AUTOMATED SYSTEMS

As libraries and their services grow and change, so do their automation needs. Evaluation of the performance of an automated system, whether it be for new purchase or ongoing refinement, can provide several useful types of management information on: (1) whether new or updated systems meet contract requirements; (2) whether the system is living up to the performance and output standards of its user community; (3) the point at which a new system or system refinements are needed; (4) possible future resource consumption.

Criteria

It is obvious that a computer system can be evaluated according to different types of criteria—ease of use, cost, reliability, integratibility, and so on. In her survey of 54 major research libraries in North America, Johnson (1991) discovered that ease of use by patrons was a major consideration in the selection of a new system—above cost and, perhaps surprisingly, ease of use by staff. The weight given to ease of use by patrons agrees with her findings that these same libraries considered improvement of user services as the major objective of automation and improved service to users as the major accomplishment of automation.

Purposes

Notably, Peters (1988) identifies three types of systems evaluation: (1) functional—to determine whether a system's features meet the library's needs; (2) economic—to determine the affordability of a system; and (3) performance—to reveal whether the system capacity can meet present or anticipated future demands. These evaluation factors interact, based on the needs, political climate, and the economics involved in a library's decision to make a new purchase or to upgrade an existing system.

Peters comments that a significant amount of importance is placed on performance evaluation due to the maturity of the library automation market place, which encourages healthy vendor competition. The reasons are numerous, but they can be grouped into two general categories, the first associated with buying or designing new systems, and the second with improving existing systems, summarized by Peters as follows:

> "We are interested in performance evaluation because we are concerned about the long-term price/performance profile of the systems we are buying. First, we are interested in assessing whether the systems we buy meet the performance requirements expressed in our contracts and regulated through our acceptance tests and system management instruments. But we are also interested in upgrading our systems. Let's face it, we all want to add more terminals, get gifts from heaven that allow our recon programmes to exceed their

most optimistic projections, and otherwise receive good news that places new demands on our library automation systems. We need to know precisely whether our existing systems can be expanded to handle the load or whether new systems will be needed. We also need to learn answers to such questions in an orderly fashion."

Here Lynch (1988) cautions that interpreting the myriad of data that systems generate in order to identify appropriate measures and criteria is neither simple nor precise, and should not be based on subjective or administratively motivated aims to justify investments or change. He points out that—one of the greatest difficulties challenging system managers of large, complex public access information retrieval systems. Where the system services a wildly varying set searches from one day to the next, is the identification of meaningful measures of system behaviour. There are obviously many possible ways in which approaches to the evaluation of automated systems can be categorized. For the purposes of this chapter, two major approaches are identified:

(i) Evaluation without user involvement or with less than full user involvement.

(ii) Evaluation with fill user involvement.

The second type assumes a fully operating system in which one can evaluate not only system characteristics per se but also how a particular community makes use of the system and with what degree of success. The other type of evaluation, while it may involve user input, is concerned with the system in a more abstract sense. Indeed, this type of evaluation may be undertaken before a system has actually been selected, before it has been accepted, or before it is fully operational. Although the terms are not completely accurate, we will refer to this class of evaluation as "user-free" and the second class as "user-involved."

User-Free Evaluation

This category of evaluation focuses on system features rather than on how these are exploited by a particular group of users. It may be used in the selection of a system, the acceptance of a system, or decisions relating to system enhancement or replacement.

One useful tool that can be used in the selection of system is a checklist to determine the features present in a particular systems or, more particularly, to compare the characteristics of two or more systems. Typically, checklists of desirable system features are developed, and evaluators study the system(s) interest, noting the presence or absence of the features under investigation, and any other pertinent information. The results are frequently entered into a grid in which marks, numeric or symbolic, indicate the presence or absence of features. A point value may be assigned to each feature, and a differential weighting scheme may be established to place emphasis on features that are considered more important than others. In other cases, features are assigned an equal rating of 1 or 0. System scores can be derived from the grids, with subtotals to indicate system strengths in particular areas, and total scores to indicate overall performance. The checklist method of evaluation is useful for several reasons. In the case of a single system review, it helps one to arrive at a list of desirable features, and to identify the strengths and weaknesses of a particular system. In the case of a multiple system review, a comparative checklist can help to verify the existence of features across systems and thus to identify comparative strengths and weaknesses. Where a weighted scoring scheme is used. One can compare several systems on the basis strengths and weaknesses in areas determined to be most important in meeting the needs of a particular library. The use of a checklist ensures that the same questions about system features are posed consistently across systems.

Weighting of system features is always desirable. Otherwise, the checklist scores can be deceptive. Without weighting, a system with many "superfluous" features may obtain a high overall score, but may actually be weak in features that librarians and users rate as most important. Similarly, a flat rating scheme may obscure the fact that a particular system is strong in features that users prefer, even though it may be lacking elsewhere. The challenge, then, lies in obtaining consensous on what weighting scheme equitably represents a library's preferences for system features, and in implementing the weighting scheme consistently. Cherry et al. (1994) employed a checklist to survey features in the OPACs of twelve Canadian academic libraries. Data on each system were collected twice, by two different researchers, and the two datasets were checked a third time against the systems to resolve any disagreements.

One hundred seventy features were included in the checklist, grouped into ten functional categories:

1. Database characteristics
2. Operational control
3. Searching
4. Subject search aids
5. Access points
6. Screen display
7. Output control
8. Commands
9. User assistance
10. OPAC usability via remote access

This checklist is unique among library-oriented checklists because it is based both on similar checklists for the study of OPAC features and a checklist designed for evaluating the usability of human-computer interfaces. It was found that most of the OPACs, as implemented in the libraries, possessed more than half the features that were listed as desirable on the checklist. All systems scored well on "screen display," and were weakest in "subject search aids," "output control," and "operational control".

Overall, Cherry et al. observe that, in spite of the many improvements in OPAC design, "... there is still a wide gap between the systems evaluated in this study and the ideal OPAC system suggested by researchers." They also recommend that the study be replicated every two to three years, and that the results in each category be compared to measure improvement in system design over time. They admit that the study would have been improved by the use of weights to reflect the relative importance of each feature, and recommend that further studies should survey online system users to determine the relative importance that they assign to specific system features.

Acceptance testing or *benchbmarking* is a process often used by libraries to verify that the new or upgraded system meets the contract requirements. Often the conditions of acceptance in a contract indicate clearly what type of performance is expected, and the acceptable level of performance, to determine whether a system works in the manner agreed upon in the contract. Although acceptance testing usually has legal implications, Lynch (1988) notes that it is difficult to bridge the gap between the contract language and the types of tests that both parties (vendor and library) agree will demonstrate whether or not the system is acceptable in all aspects. An interesting series of three articles tracks the experience of Boston University's stress test with a particular system, providing perspectives from a librarian, the system designer, and a consultant. Brown (1988) presents the library's perspective on stress tests designed to determine system performance at a 100-terminal capacity.

The results indicated that immediate improvements needed

to be made by the vendor; they also suggested more realistic testing parameters acceptable to both parties. Brown believes that acceptance testing may need to be made an actual part of a contract. Salmon (1988), representing the perspective of the systems designer, points out some of the unrealistic conditions that drove the strees test, although those conditions did not appear overly demanding in the contract language.

Epstein (1988), the consultant for the project, focused on response time concerns, emphasizing the importance of distinguishing between response time and throughput of actual transactions to achieve the most direct searching and retrievel results for users. He also pointed out that the significant cost of acceptance testing causes vendors to enter into it only when they are interested in upscaling their operations to larger or more complex systems. In recent years, acceptance testing has evolved into a more feasible part of systems implementation. More emphasis on trials of system performance with realistic usage loads and operating environments has succeeded in making acceptance testing less a politically and emotionally charged conflict between library and vendor and more a productive collaboration for their mutual benefit.

Once installed, monitoring of the ongoing performance of a system is crucial to the detection of subtle problems or system degradation. The installation of changes, including addition of new components, necessitates checking not only the new portion of the system, but the interaction between that and existing modules and programmes. Ongoing monitoring of system performance usually takes place in the form of regularly generated system reports. Libraries typically review response time, input/ out-put information, and network throughput on a regular basis for signals of system degradation in any one or a combination of these areas. In the case of response time, several authors have emphasized the need to perform careful ongoing system analysis before concluding that poor or decreased response time is attributable to any one factor. It is usually the case that several factors contribute to system performance degradation.

When system changes or new features are added, the acceptance or stress test is normally used to evaluate the system under various conditions. Libraries, usually in consultation with vendors, develop scripts of search commands and strategies that are executed during a set period of time by an agreed upon number of participants stationed at terminals in predetermined locations. At times, public or staff users identify problems or make suggestions for system changes designed to refine its operation or its interaction with users. The feedback for making these changes can come from word of mouth or from the periodic review of performance logs generated by the system. For instance, librarians may observe searches failing at a critical point where the insertion of an automatically invoked help screen could render assistance. Similarly, a new version of the system software may be installed periodically, usually containing code that tunes or refines existing features.

When changes are made to features of functions within an existing system, some means are needed to test how well these changes work. Stress tests are commonly used to test implementations of new features.

Capactiy planning is another important element in overall evaluation. The timely allocation of resources to support the growth of a system is critical to its continued optimum performance. By tracking the size of the database, and estimating its growth rate, projections can be made about when to increase capacity, and whether this increase in size will degrade or otherwise affect response time and other performance factors. Precise capacity planning is difficult because it involves projection and prediction based on numerous complex performance factors. Lynch (1988) claims that capacity planning "usually involves a good deal of inspired guesswork."

Unless there is a clear understanding of how all performance factors interact on a day-to-day basis, it is difficult to predict how they will interact in the future, given the introduction of increased, new, or different uses of the system. Schmidt and Pobuda (1988) developed a capacity planning model for the RLIN system that they used to support hardware upgrades to the CPU. The information used in the model was based primarily on the number and types of transactions made, the resources required to process these transactions, and the "varieties in the mix of transactions over time." They obtained projections from RLIN users of the amount of cataloging, interlibrary loan, acquisitions, and reference use they would make during the time period in question. These projections, as well as actual usage statistics for the three previous years, were analyzed using a PC spreadsheet programme that was capable of time-series analysis. Schmidt and Pobuda's model makes projections for "budgeted activity" and "maximum activity". These on projected activity are then translated into projected system resource utilization.

Projected resource utilization is further divided into several categories to take into consideration not only maximum projected usage, but also the projected usage during peak system load periods, which are defined as the busiest times of the day when libraries in all time zones were using RLIN. In order to validate their model, they compared their projections with an actual response time graph of the RLIN CPU that occurred during FY 1987, and obtained a fairly close matchup. Capacity planning models can be implemented within a library environment through a combination of the informa-tion generated regularly by most online systems and the statistics normally collected within the library. Changes in transaction volume during peak and other usage times can signal the need for system expansion, involving the addition of various hardware and software resources.

First, steady increases over time in the overall system usage, especially the number of simultaneous system transactions, can signal the need to increase system capacity. Secondly, increases in the aggregate numbers of transactions at specific locations can serve as indicators for a need to add more terminals. Capacity planning has yet another facet—planning for the provision of adequate access to the online system whether through onsite terminals or remotely. Determining whether the number of physical connections to the system adequately supports the library's user base is an important component of planning.

A review of system resources exploited by various user group, and in specific locations, can assist in providing this information. Several studies have employed queuing theory in analyzing the frequency of terminal usage, and determining how many and where to place terminals. It is important to examine where increases in usage are occurring by user type, with public, staff, dial, or network access.

User-Involved Evaluation

For over twenty years, a growing body of research base on information science and cognitive psychology has been performed to gain a better understanding of how users interact with systems, and how the results of that interaction can be evaluated. One practical goal of this type of research is to collect and analyze information that can be fed back into better system design. A growing body of literature in this area places heavy emphasis on the central role of the end user in the evaluation process. Benefits include the ability of librarians and systems designers to view the use of a system from a perspective that they, for all their technical or content knowledge, could not anticipate.

Obvious drawbacks arise with data collection and analysis that does not include a group or groups that are representative of a system's actual user population. The interaction between the user and the system can be the subject of study for a number of purposes. The studies discussed in this chapter are carried out to learn more about how a system is used and to improve its performance. Many possible methods are applicable. Unobtrusive measures gather data while library patrons are actually using the system.

Users may or may not be aware that their keystrokes, or other actions, are being recorded or observed. The methods are unobtrusive in the sense that users are not being asked any questions and are not required to do anything they would not otherwise be doing. Obtrusive measures are used primarily to obtain feedback on user preferences for various system features and their opinions on system performance. A primary goal of unobtrusive measurement is to be able to record and evaluate user activity in a natural environment without intervention from the researcher.

Data thus collected can be useful in revealing how specific system features are exploited and in identifying features that appear to be giving users significant problems. At least three types of approach are applicable: review of transaction logs, direct observation of users operating at terminals, and video and/or audio taping of user performance. Unobtrusive data can be used to re-create exactly what occurred in a patron's encounter with the system and can complement more subjective data gathered form library users. Nielsen (1986) points out that differences may exist between what users say has happened and what actually occurred as determined by a more objective observation of their behaviour.

Transaction log analysis (TLA) has been defined as the "...study of electronically recorded interactions between online information retrieval systems and the persons who search for the information found in those systems" (Peters et al., 1993a). After its initial application in the 1960s as a tool for evaluating system performance, transaction log analysis gathered momentum in the 1970s and 1980s as a means of analyzing the interaction between users and online catalogs. Peters (1993) lists approximately ninety studies of online systems that, since 1980, have employed TLA although he points out that relatively few researchers have performed more than one study (see also the bibliography by Peters et al., 1993b).

Many TLA studies gather information on how frequently system features are used: choice of search type, use of help screens, how may hits users are willing to review, how often a search results in zero hits, the number and type of error messages that users receive, and so on. A few studies have employed TLA in conjunction with other methods to examine the affective and cognitive searching behaviour of user interaction with online systems (Tenopir et al., 1989). OPAC transaction logs to show the types of data that can be collected (Flaherty, 1993). Several studies have analyzed user errors in searching online systems and have suggested system changes or enhancements that would assist in avoiding the occurrence of these errors. Dickson (1984), in an early analysis of user errors in searching an OPAC, found that a significant number of searches failed through a combination of spelling errors, the omission of initial articles from title searches and failure to invert surnames. Jones (1986) used TLA to identify such problems as keying errors (typographical errors, or putting information in the wrong place), slow response time for known item searches, and problems following the general search path structure.

Walker and Jones (1987) tested two versions of an OPAC at two different locations. One version contained additional features that provided for automatic stemming, spelling correction, and cross-reference tables to enhance subject retrieval. They found that neither group of users was aware of the corrective features that had been installed in one of the test systems, even though searching failures had decreased there. Peters (1989) used transaction logs to examine "no-hit" search results, finding that 39 percent of the items sought were not owned by the library and 21 percent of the failures occurring were the result of typographical errors.

Flaherty (1990), in an examination of the reasons for search failures, tested the value of automatic space adjustment, automatic term flip (word order correction), soundex, and a spell checker, and found that the introduction of these features could correct 63 percent of the "no-hit" search failures that occurred in the OPAC. The results of these studies have yielded a set of commonly recognized system problems, many of which have been remedied by most vendors and system designers. TLA has also been employed to determine implications for bibliographic instruction programmes and further system enhancement and design. Wallace (1993) studied transaction logs of eleven public access terminals in an academic library and found that the use of system-supplied help varied, that a high percentage of subject keyword searches produced ten or fewer hits, that users persist in scanning lists of titles, even in searches with large retrievals, and that system design improvements need to be complemented by increased emphasis on searching skills in bibliographic instruction programmes.

An annotated bibliography by Peters et al. (1993b) and a review article by Simpson (1989) serve as two excellent sources of further information about TLA. Borgman et al. (1996) provide a valuable and thorough discussion of online monitoring as a research method based on extensive experience with an online catalog for children. Commercially available systems offer various logging features examples of a "no hits" report and of use of author names in an OPAC.

Despite all of its potential benefits, transaction log analysis does have limitations. In many systems with transaction log monitoring facilities, it is either difficult or impossible to delineate individual user searching sessions. Further, the transaction log is only able to show the "footprints" of the user on the system—it cannot provide an explanation for why a searcher made the search choices that are reflected in the transaction log. It has also been shown that it is difficult to perform transaction log analysis across systems.

Another problem is that of cost. A comprehensive monitoring module can add a significant overhead to the cost of operating the system. Some institutions, including libraries, have discontinued use of such modules because of the additional cost of applying them and because of the fact that library managers lacked time to analyze the data on a regular basis. Transaction log analysis collects data about system use in the aggregate and deals only with the quantitative—which commands are used how often, which headings are consulted, how much time is spent per session, and so on. But more individualized and qualitative data can also be obtained unobtrusively online. The most obvious example is the monitoring and analysis of use of a *help* command. Knowing what types of help are requested by users, especially in the case of a new system or one that has recently added new features, can be of great value in identifying problem areas that may not have been anticipated in the system design but may, in fact, be rather easy to correct.

Although it is rarely acknowledge, *direct observation* is perhaps one of the most commonly employed techniques for collecting information about online system users. Critics often suggest that observation is an unscientific way of gathering only the information needed to support one's own views. The technique need not be flawed; it is the degree of consistency in what is observed, and at what intervals it is observed, that determines the reliability of the data collected. Observation of user behaviour at online terminals is perhaps the easiest technique to employ because it is often a mere extension of a librarian's responsibilities in a reference or other public service setting. Observation is often the technique employed in queuing studies to determine the number of terminals that are needed in certain areas to support an optimal level of access at peak usage times.

It is important to employ valid sampling techniques in conjunction with observation in order to obtain reliable data on which management decisions can be based. For example, if one wants to know how many times users have to wait in line to use terminals in the reference room, one obviously cannot rely solely on the observations of a single librarian who only staffs the reference desk fifteen hours per week, between 8 a.m. and 5 p.m., Monday through Friday. Direct observation can be useful, on its own or to supplement other methods, when appropriate sampling methods are employed and input is received from more than one observer.

A number of studies have analyzed the results of *video and/ or audio taping* of the speech and actions of users during search sessions. The technique has been used to examine whether the cognitive, affective, or attitudinal behaviour or users affects their performance and the outcomes of searching. Methods like protocol analysis, which employ a per-determined framework for analyzing user comments (asking a user to "think aloud" while searching, then recording the resulting behaviour and comments), can be used to classify and evaluate the relative effect of user decision-making and behaviour on the success or failure of searching. Janosky et al. (1986) performed one of the first studies of this kind applied to an OPAC.

Their subjects, university students, were given several searching tasks to perform. Their "thinking aloud" was recorded on tape and their interactions with the system were captured and analyzed in order to identify types of errors made. Tenopir et al. (1991) employed audio taping, in addition to transaction log analysis, in their study of users who were searching a full-text database of magazine articles. They found that users pursued mainly "single-minded" search strategies. Sandore and Ryan (1994) employed audio taping, a survey questionnaire, TLA, and the method of protocol analysis to analyze the activity of searchers of a journal citation database. They found that users who encountered zero or one-hit retrievals often commented that they felt their searching skills and/or subject knowledge to be inadequate to undertake the searching task.

Survey questionnaires enable the collection of data about user satisfaction with a system or specific aspects of it, searching preferences and attitudes, demographic data about users, and the level of skills or knowledge that users possess. Questionnaire surveys involve contact with users; therefore, the evaluator must share with the user some information, however brief, regarding the intent of the survey, how the data will be analyzed and used, and what steps the library has taken to insure that no data will be used in such a way that it reveals the identity of individual users. The published literature includes several studies in which online questionnaires were applied to record user attitudes and preferences for system features, or to make possible a "critical incident" approach to studying searches recently completed by users. Two such studies were completed using the University of California MELVYL system. The first, by Larson and Graham (1983), linked transaction log data to online questionnaires to determine what proportion of the searches performed were subject searches.

Horres et al. (1991) used a combination of two online questionnaires, transaction logs, and a printed questionnaire to analyze user satisfaction with the MELVYL implementation of MEDLINE at several campuses. System designers wanted feedback from users on general satisfaction with the system and on the use of specific system features. Both online questionnaires used only multiple choice questions. The first received a 45% response rate, and the second, applied one year later, a 33% response rate.

The printed questionnaire, used to supplement the online questionnaires by collecting open-ended comments, had a response rate of 73%. The evaluation results reported high satisfaction with and high overall use of the system. The questionnaires and the review of the transaction logs also revealed that many of the advanced searching features were rarely used. Effects on library services were also measured, and these included significant increases in reference transactions and interlibrary loan requests, with a significant decline in mediated search services.

Hancock-Beaulieu et al. (1990) describe online system evaluation using OLIVE, an interactive front-end system, which enables the collection of transaction log data, full-screen logging of search sessions, administering of online and offline questionnaires, and interactive questionnaires during search sessions, at specified points. Belkin et al. (1990) employ a combination of transaction log analysis, online questionnaires, observation, and interviews in their study to assess goals, tasks, and behaviour of users of libraries and online catalogs. A modified version of the OLIVE front-end software is employed in their study. Sandore and Ryan (1994) administered an online questionnaire for a critical incident study of searching and to measure the working knowledge of library users on the logical elements of online bibliographic searching.

Notably, the advantage of online questionnaires over printed questionnaires is the ability to collect critical incident data about a search session immediately following the session. Response rates in the range of 30-45%, reported in some studies, are comparable to response rates for many surveys using printed questionnaires. Online questionnaires remove the problems associated with distribution and return of the instruments by mail or by other means. In comparison with questionnaires and transaction log analysis, *interviews* can provide a more intimate view of the user's perspective on the system under examination. Interviews may be conducted on a one-to-one basis, either over the telephone or face to face.

They can be structured, with specific questions and pre-specified categories in which to slot answers, or unstructured, with open-ended questions that provide the subjects with more opportunity to provide unsolicited information about the system. A study by Nitecki (1993) to identify a taxonomy of user criteria for evaluating the effectiveness of an online catalog employed unstructured interviews and used a qualitative approach in analyzing the resulting information.

Another type of interview—the focus group interview-may be conducted with a small group and one or more interviewers, with video and/or audio taping, and/or assistants transcribing notes and statements during the group discussion. Focus group interviews are regularly used in marketing research to gather information from a particular, per-selected group of users about products or potential products. The emphasis in the focus group interview rests with identifying the range of attitudes or opinions from a group of users who have certain demographic or otherwise significant points in common (gender, socio-economic status, race, age) about a series of questions related to system use. This technique helps to identify characteristics of identifiable user groups, along with attitudes. Researchers working on the NSF/ARPA/NASA-funded Digital Library Initiative at the University of Illinois have carried out focus group interviews with engineering faculty and students to determine what features they felt were important to include in a digital library for an engineering community. Further, they observed the online searching behaviour of patrons working in the University of Illinois Grainger Engineering Library, noting that users experienced difficulty searching existing systems (Sandusky, 1995). The Illinois research team used this information to design a transaction log that will track the searches performed on the trstbed for the project—the full text of over twenty engineering journals (Sandusky, 1996).

This work is significant from the standpoint that it will enable the unobtrusive study of specific uses of networked information. Some online systems offer the option for users to send *unsolicited comments* to librarians or system designers. In some cases, system administrators post an e-mail address to encourage users to report bugs or anomalies they encounter while searching the system. Some of these anomalies may be bibliographic in nature—typographical errors in the bibliographic record—or related to cataloging policy. Other anomalies, such as screens that are missing placeholders or are incorrectly formatted, may not be discovered in the regular system beta testing or debugging process.

Therefore, the comment option is a valuable tool in problem identification. Pennsylvania State University's LIAS online catalog was one of the first systems to offer the "oops" command, which users could invoke in order to send a brief message reporting either system or bibliographic anomalies to the systems and library staff. Current systems commonly offer an option that enables users to send mail messages from within the system to system administrators or other staff who work closely with various aspects of the catalog. For over a decade the library of the University of Illinois at Urbana-Champaign has maintained a user comment box in the public catalog area of the main library. Users regularly deposit recommended corrections for typographical errors to bibliographic records, suggestions for adding subject or name headings to particular records in order to enhance access, or general recommendations about other system needs. Once a month a librarian reviews the comments and forwards them to staff in appropriate units or to an online system advisory committee for appropriate action.

Various system enhancements have been made as a result of comments received in this way. In any study that elicits specific information about use of an online system, it is important at the outset to provide the user with a written statement on the institution's policy regarding human subjects research. Those conducting the study must do everything possible to ensure that the publicly-available results of the analysis will not disclose the identity of an individual user, or link that user with information specific to his or her information-seeking behaviour.

Analysis of the use of online *help* features was mentioned earlier as an unobtrusive source of information on problems encountered by users. But users can also go to members of the library staff when they need help, and their interactions with staff members is a further source of information on system problems and weaknesses. Many public service departments maintain statistics on the types of reference and other assistance they provide to users, including online system assistance. A recent study of the impact of locally mounted periodical citation databases on library staff, users, and collections at the University of Illinois revealed a decrease in patron assistance in locating journals, since the new system supplied call numbers and library locations with the journal citations.

Further, it is noteworthy that Online system advisory groups or committees are often appointed to advise library administrators and system designers on what the groups feel should be the development priorities. Frequently they are organized with the intention that the appointees represent, in the organization's policy and operational matters, the perceived needs of both the librarian and user populations.

The groups can also provide a forum for staff input on design and problem issues. If a computer center supports the library's online system, the inclusion of one or more representatives from this center maintains a direct channel of communication concerning developmental and organizational priorities between those who design and maintain the system and those who use it. Groups charged with providing advice on the implementation of online systems may be developed on the basis of need. For example, an ad hoc implementation group might be appointed to assist in the implementation of a new module of an integrated system. Groups of this type have a limited and focused charge, and normally dissolve or, if needed, are reconstituted into a permanent committee once their initial work is accomplished.

Committees and working groups serve the valuable function of providing advice to administrators regarding policy and operational matters related to running online systems in a manner that is effective for users, both within and beyond the library's walls.

Limitations

No doubt, the reasons for performance evaluation are compelling, much of the work done in systems evaluation within libraries is the exception rather than the rule. This situation can be commonly observed for a number of reasons. Sometimes system resource usage is neither the concern nor the domain of the library, but rather of the campus or city administrative computing center. In situations where the management of the computing facilities is separated from the management of the library, it is more difficult to establish a cohesive picture of the factors that affect the system's performance, much less to correct these situations when performance problems arise.

Also, online systems typically generate hundreds of statistical reports about the system functions on a regular (usually monthly) basis. Often, information about system resources usage needs to be carefully analyzed and translated to adifferent format in order to be usable for library managers. System vendors have moved increasingly to report generation modules that can be customized by libraries in order to avoid this pitfall. The analysis of system performance data requires both skill and a commitment to ongoing analysis.

Not all librarians feel they have adequate training in the use of quantitative or qualitative analysis method. Further, it is not always clear where in the library organization the responsibility ought to rest for ongoing evaluation beyond the annual budgeting process for equipment, software, and online contractual services. The published literature reveals that this analysis is now being performed by many different people-systems, reference, collection development, technical services, and administrative librarians.

The developments discussed in some of the earlier chapters strongly suggest that the library of the future will be dealing more and more with information resources that are network-accessible and less and less with those owned as physical artifacts. Although the evaluation of library services per se is outside the scope of the present book (the subject is covered in detail in Lancaster, 1993a, and Baker and Lancaster, 1991) it is appropriate to consider in what way the evaluation of such a "digital library" may differ from the evaluation of the more traditional library.

Traditional models for evaluating library services are largely based on whether or not the library, its resources and its tools can assist users to find the items or information they need. Technology has enabled libraries to expand access to information resources beyond the physical walls, both for library staff and for users. In some cases this has meant that the library no longer plays the role of intermediary in the delivery of information. As the locus of information resources traditionally associated with a trip to the library becomes increasingly decentralized and remotely accessible, the role of the library in providing these services will inevitably change.

So too will the library's ability to evaluate its performance directly. How will the traditional model change as we move increasingly into a digital and networked environment, where users have direct access to remote infor-mation, and rely less often on the library and its resources for answers to their questions? What will become the role of the library as we now know it, with its quantifiable resources and collections?

How can the library use technology to understand the needs of library users more completely, both in the traditional and the evolving digital library setting? A model that depicts the most important current components of traditional library evaluation, and how they are employed. This traditional evaluation model has identifiable components, such as user characteristics, reasons for using the library, the size of the library collection, staff efficiency and accuracy, and whether user needs are satisfied within the necessary time frame. Characteristics, behaviour, and needs of users can now be observed, to some extent at least, because most of the services offered by traditional libraries require that the user enter the library at some point to receive them. Little is known of the characteristics, behaviour, and needs of nonusers in most communities. The input predictors of the library's performance include the size of the general and reference collections and the rate at which new materials are added.

Within the library, the interactions among staff processes, the library's resources and tools, and the user processes combine to produce outputs and, ultimately, outcomes. Measures of output and outcome indicate whether the information or item was obtained, whether used, and whether it had short-term (ST) or long-term (LT) impacts on the user. The most obvious output predictors of performance are circulation, number of reference questions answered, and number of literature searches performed. Libraries normally collect these data on a regular basis, either manually or through electronic monitoring. Such data quantify the services provided. True output measures relate to the effectiveness of the work done, in terms of correctness, timeliness, desired amount, and so on. While commonly accepted output measures exist (e.g., shelf availability), they require some effort to apply. Outcomes are rarely looked at: very little is known about what use is made of publications or information after users leave the library.

Some changes are needed in order to build a working model for evaluation in a digital library environment. *First,* it is clear that user groups will change, as will the library's ability to monitor their needs and behaviours. Since users will no longer need to come to the library to obtain access to library materials, they will be more remote, and more anonymous. It is likely that the group of users may widen to include previous non-users.

This could occur because the library may provide convenient or costeffective electronic access to information that formerly was not available in the library, or because the resources are now perceived to be more accessible than they were before.

Secondly, the purposes for which users seek information may change in the digital library environment. Users will have access to the electronic tools needed to build and organize their own databases of information, to create new documents incorporating or referring to that information and to find people to communicate with or to collaborate with on future projects.

Thirdly, the role of the library in information provision will change, although it is too soon to determine in what ways, and to what degree these changes will occur. In a networked environment, a library may become merely a switching center, a switching center providing valueadded interfaces and indices to electronic information, or a database builder, selecting electronic information of greatest interest to users and building databases incorporating that information.

Ultimately, and perhaps most obviously, the nature of the library's "collection" will change. Resources are becoming more dispersed and intangible as the concept of a collection beyond the library's physical walls is extended. The nature of the library's "control" over the contents of these collections is also changing. Items in collections, once considered discrete pieces of information, are developing fuzzy boundaries, due to the ability of authors and users to provide hypermedia links among textual and other items in a networked digital environment. Documents can now be dynamic and interactive in nature, and may not be printable. The content of collections, or items within collections, may also change rapidly. It is clear that such yardsticks as size of collection or number of items acquired annually have little meaning for the digital library. Also of little meaning are all output measures that relate to ownership of physical items, "shelf availability" being perhaps the most obvious example. Presumably, "items accessed" replaces "circulation" as a quantitative measure of use.

However, if the actions of users can be monitored (some form of transaction logging as discussed earlier), finer measure of use become possible: how much text is accessed, how much is merely viewed, how much is downloaded to personal databases, and so an. The fact that many users will be "remote" and "anonymous" makes evaluation more difficult. The fact that some of their actions are susceptible to monitoring makes some types of evaluation easier to implement If the digital library is used for the same purposes as the traditional library—to find a particular item, to find the answer to a question, to find information on a particular subject-the evaluation criteria also remain more or less the same.

Nevertheless, the digital library may present special problems in evaluation, as suggested earlier; e.g., "items" may have rather fuzzy boundaries and some text may lack stability (databases, and perhaps even individual items, may be updated frequently). If the digital library is used for other purposes—e.g., to build composite documents from several sources scattered throughout the network, to locate people with similar interests, and so on—different evaluation criteria will be needed. In a highly developed digital information network, one can visualize a situation in which a scholar builds a personal database by downloading from network resources the text and graphics of most direct interest.

This scholar may be supported by some form of institutional library (maintained perhaps by a university, college, or company) which has also downloaded from the broader network the text and graphics most likely to be of value to the institutional community. If an important role of the institutional library is to "feed" the personal databases of its users in a dynamic way (e.g., through some form of profile matching), the most obvious evaluation criterion would relate to the frequency with which an individual needs to go beyond personal and institutional resources to satisfy a particular need. Presumably, if the institutional library was doing an excellent job, most of the individual's needs would be satisfied from his/her own database, some from the institutional database, and very little from the wider network resources.

The digital library environment is one in which there is a high level of interaction between users and documents and perhaps between users and users. The fundamental definitions of traditional terms used to describe the library's role in information organization and delivery are being challenged, and institutional boundaries are becoming fuzzy.

Many communities are developing their own databases of organized information resources in ways that enable them to access and manipulate this information optimally. Emphasis in data sharing is placed on the most convenient format for the user's needs, as opposed to the standard data formats that libraries employ in order to facilitate data exchange.

The term "library" is being extended in the metaphoric sense, to the point where it will not simply refer to the traditional physical structures and collections organized and managed by library professionals. In the most basic sense, users are the builders of their own digital information environment. Whereas the traditional library enables users to interact simultaneously with the same materials at one physical point in time, the digital library increases the opportunities for users to make serial as well as synchronous use of the same materials in digital format, as well as enabling them to communicate with each other about the material at hand.

The development of digital libraries is accompanied by a multi-disciplinary interest in evaluation. Evaluation in the six NSF/ARPA/NASA- sponsored Digital Library Initiative projects incorporates qualitative methods developed by researchers from various fields— sociology, phycology, communications, computer science, and engineering (URL-http: // dli. grainger. uiuc. edu/ national. htm). Researchers in these projects are working to find out what are the most significant factors affecting use of electronic information in various areas of activity. Online system transaction monitoring is being employed widely to study the searching patterns of users, along with interviews, questionnaires, video taping, and other methods.

5

MAIN ELEMENTS OF ELECTRONIC LIBRARIES

LIBRARIES AND THE INTERNET

Internet is now a popular mode of communication and knowledge dissemination. The Internet is arguably the electronic resource that is now having the most significant impact on library services and operations and on the professional activities of librarians. This strength of impact is due to its multifaceted nature since it simultaneously fulfils three important roles in library services. First, it is a resource that can be consulted· and used like any other reference tool. Second, it is more dynamic and far-reaching than any other resource used in a library setting. Finally, it provides a medium of communication that has extended the potential of librarians for interaction beyond the physical library (to users, colleagues, and other professionals), beyond any previous capacity, and in a host of new ways. This chapter explores the impact of the Internet on library services, professional activities, and relationships with library users. The Internet is actually a non-network. It is technically comprised of a group of high-speed computer networks that are interconnected by the use of a common communications protocol-TCP/IP (transmission control protocol/Internet protocol). The theoretical simplicity of this scheme, plus the rapid decrease in the cost of computing technology, have contributed to the widespread growth of connectivity to the Internet. What began as a high-speed network linking

Department of Defence centres in the late 1960s has grown into a multipurpose public communication/information vehicle, currently with very few formal restrictions on content and purpose.

A concise but rather complete description of the Internet and its resources has been provided by the Library Association (1995):

> The Internet consists of a large number of linked computer networks forming a global network. This is largely open and free, allowing users to communicate with each other for work and recreational purposes, and for corporate and personal reasons. Because the Internet is so vast and is without regulation or hierarchy, the network is a treasure-trove of information from many sources. Resources are available in all subjects; mailing is possible for all the participants; documents can be forwarded and delivered across the world; and directories and journals abound. Developments such as the World Wide Web combine friendliness of user interface with enormously powerful information retrieval capability. Electronic mail is one of the most important services offered through the Internet, with each person having a personal mail address, enabling them to link up to another user anywhere in the world and communicate within seconds.

Remarkably, late 1991, the High Performance Computing Act, signed into law by President Bush, authorized the establishment of the National Research and Education Network (NREN). Although libraries are specifically mentioned in few areas of this legislation, the context suggests that libraries and information services were intended to comprise a part of the network (Mc Clure et al., 1992).

On March 21, 1994 Vice President Gore addressed the International Telecommunications Union meeting, exhorting the participants to support work on building the Global Information Infrastructure (GII):

> The president and I have called for positive government action in the United States to extend the NII to every classroom, library, hospital, and clinic in the U.S. by the end of the century. I want to urge that this conference include in its agenda for action the commitment to determine how every school and library in every country can be connected to the Internet, the world's largest computer network, in order to create a Global Digital Library. (Gore, 1994, page 813)

It is important to recognize that the Internet's vast capability to enable the sharing of data is largely due to the efforts of individuals or groups to provide software or data files for public consumption, free or at a low cost. This "grass roots" development spirit, and U.S. government funding, is largely responsible for the availability of such a wealth of information. By the same token, this loosely coordinated growth and duplication has created one of the most complex retrieval challenges to users of online systems.

Early work by Lynch and Preston (1990) describes the resources available at that time through the Internet, and discusses the proposed impact on library services and user behaviour. Within a relatively short period of time, libraries and librarians have integrated the use of the Internet into nearly all aspects of current library activities, including :

1. Communication among staff, or with colleagues or patrons, through e-mail (Cromer and Johnson, 1994); collaborative research and publication can be one facet of this (Tillman and Ladner, 1994);
2. Discussion through listservs or other electronic vehicles; this includes using the Internet to share information about the Internet itself;
3. Support of reference services of all types through search of remote databases (Ladner and Tillman, 1993) and

through a cooperative approach to the answering of "difficult" questions (Batt, 1996b);

4. Exploiting the catalogs of other institutions, which may offer access points or search features not available locally (Drabenstott and Cochrane, 1994);
5. Gathering information from library users in order to create SDI profiles for them.
6. Interlibrary loan verification, requests, document delivery, and consortial file-sharing (e-journals, images, data, and text file FTP sites);
7. Cataloging;
8. Book/Journal ordering;
9. Evaluation of competing online systems for purpose of selection;
10. Making locally-produced databases accessible to remote users;
11. Establishing home pages to provide information on the library, its resources, and its services (Branse et al., 1996).

Besides above, some organizations have formed their own internal networks, modelled on Internet principles and often connected to the Internet. Such "intranets" can be exploited by libraries to make information and resources available (West, 1997). Several print and electronic journals, newsletters, and listservs are now devoted to use of the Internet and its resources by librarians. The SUNY/OCLC *Internet Homesteader* (1994 on) claims as its mission: "bringing information available on the Internet to individuals with no Internet access and assisting those with access in finding their way." It typically includes a section for those with no Internet access that provides synopses of information from e-conferences and other library and technology-related Internet resources, as well as a section with reviews and training-related information for those with Internet access.

The contents of this newsletter provide a particularly good example of the importance that the library profession has begun to assign to professional communication using the Internet. The synopses of e-conferences give those without Internet access the opportunity to follow in print what their colleagues have deemed important professional exchange about current issues in librarianship.

In the first "Internet Librarian" column in *American Libraries,* Schneider (1995) highlights the numerous efforts of librarians to provide organizational and access tools for Internet resources. At the 1995 annual meeting of the American Library Association, the Internet Room, which has been sponsored for several years to provide Internet access for conference-goers, was moved to the center of the exhibit hall. This is an indicator not only of the popularity of network access, but also of the growing importance librarians place on access to electronic communication to support their professional activities. An exploratory study by Mc Clure et al. (1992) discusses key factors that affect public library use of networked resources and the potential roles for public libraries in the networked environment. The top four needs identified by public library respondents in their questionnaire survey were:

1. Awareness of what is available on the Internet;
2. Widespread library connectivity to the Internet;
3. Training in network navigational skills for librarians;
4. Librarian involvement in contributing to and organizing information on the Internet.

The involvement of librarians and other information professionals in training for Internet use and in the organization of information to be used on the Internet has also increased markedly. Daniel Dern, a noted technical and networking expert, perhaps anticipated the extent of librarian involvement with the Internet when he remarked that the Internet is "the librarians' full employment act of the 1990s" (Snyder, 1994).

Getting connected to the Internet has been easier for academic and government libraries than it has for public and rural libraries, where connectivity has been a major stumbling block to Internet use. Boyce and Boyce (1995) indicate that rural library out reach programmes could be greatly facilitated by Internet access such as that made available by Freenets. Holt (1995b) reinforces their point and asserts that the Internet is helping rural libraries redefine their concept of traditional limited access - "computers and networks can help rural libraries act like big libraries on a limited budget. "McClure et al. (1994) recommend that public libraries coordinate their networking activities, including OCLC, regional, and national access to networked information.

Since the early 1995 privatization of the Internet, opportunities for connectivity have expanded considerably, with fierce competition in the commercial sector to market Internet services to businesses, not-for-profit organizations, and individuals. The leading vendors of online catalog systems have developed modules that incorporate Internet and Web access, including their own customized browsers. In a study of Internet connectivity costs for public libraries, McClure et al. (1995) explore five representative connectivity models that range from single workstation, single library, to multiple workstations, multiple libraries, and multimedia systems. For example, charges for a public library to connect a single workstation with text-based capabilities to the Internet are reported at a one-time cost of $1,475, with a recurring annual cost of $12,635. The study discusses costs for hardware, software, varying levels and methods of Internet connectivity, and the accompanying training and human resources support. This study presents a useful foundation that library managers can employ to establish an overview of what their investment in Internet connectivity could provide for their users.

Impact on Library Services

Basic Internet services enable on to accomplish a number of networked information functions: connect with other computers, including library catalogs; move files of text and data using FTP commands; send and receive electronic mail; read news from many different sources; find software; search indexed databases; search for someone. Krol (1994) provides an excellent guide and resource catalog with extensive background on how these services can be used. The application of Internet services is evolving so rapidly that there is little point in providing details on specific services for functions. Liu's (1995) classified bibliography is a useful resource that examines the impact of the Internet on almost all aspects of librarianship. However, it is important to supplement print resources with information from most current discussions and documents that are available only through listservs, File Transfer Protocol (FTP) archives, and the World Wide Web (WWW), and only in electronic format.

Through access to these services, librarians have found new ways to store, move, find, and communicate about information among themselves and with users. For reference and public service librarians, this access has created many new and different service options. Kluegel's (1995) example of a search in a German online catalog through the Internet demostrates the vast time savings possible when a librarian or user connects to a remote network to verify the existence and location of a resource. Dalrymple and Roderer (1994) characterize the Inernet as "the most significant telecommunications advance affecting online searching ..." in the period of time covered by their review article -1987-1994.

Ready reference can be performed with even greater speed since materials such as dictionaries, census information U.S. government documents, and the *CIA World Fact Book* are freely available from numerous sites (Lanier and Wilkins, 1994). Locating information through the Internet remains a challenge. Access is achieved initially through "browsers," such as the Netscape Navigator and the Mircrosoft Explorer, which lead to various "search engines" that have different capabilities and purposes and operate in different ways. A search on the same topic may give very different results when a user moves from one search engine to another. This whole area is changing very rapidly, with new developments occurring on almost a daily basis. "Metasearch engines" now allow searching using several search engines simultaneously and several" intelligent agents" have been developed to perform various functions for individual users (e.g., watch for new items of a particular type or automatically create specialized databases). Torok (1997) gives an excellent picture of capabilities as of September, 1996. To aid libraries and other organizations in maintaining consistent user access to Web pages that may change physical location, OCLC has established a service called PURL (Persistent Uniform Resource Locator). Once an institution has registered its URLs (Uniform Resource Locators—the Web address of a document) with the PURL service, software freely distributed by OCLC helps Web managers to keep track of any subsequent address changes so that the user who returns to a URL that has been changed will be seamlessly routed to the new URL (OCLC Makes PURL ..., 1996). Lanier and Wilkins note that the availability of electronic versions of print resources, as well as electronic-only sources, has increased pressure of reference librarians to stay current with Internet resources, but has also increased the likelihood that users will not leave the reference desk empty-handed. They urge that reference librarians must continue to develop their roles as "intermediaries" in the information-seeking process.

Abels and Liebscher (1994) are studying the way in which electronic reference provision is changing the nature of traditional reference interaction with users. Information professionals beyond the library have a keen interest in the development of software tools that have indexed the Web. A recent review of Web indexes places over thirty-five such tools in eight different categories, depending on the type of information desired: search engines; directories, "whats new" - sites that index Web pages that have recently been added; e-mail address finders; gopher archives; software search engines; newsgroup search engines, and metasearch engines (Conte,1996).

The Internet has contributed to the creation of a new information environment— the digital library. At the base of the digital library is the capability to retrieve, manage, store, and publish information in numerous formats. Lucier (1995) describes an effort to build a digital library for the health sciences (DLHS) at the University of California, San Francisco. He suggests that the current structure of print-based libraries that integrate electronic resources is not sufficient to support a true digital library. He views the DLHS objectives as driven primarily by the expectations of its users, and suggests that it has three primary roles:

1. information storage, retrieval, and preservation;
2. information access and delivery;
3. the online publishing of biomedical knowledge (knowledge management)

Although these roles are consistent with current information transfer principles, Lucier emphasizes that the DLHS is not the

> ...exclusive performer of these roles. In many functions, the DLHS plays a minor role, while other collaborators, such as publishers and individual scientists, make more significant contributions. However, the DLHS adds value in partnership with others through every step of this cycle. (Page 348)

To accomplish this evolution to a digital library, Lucier outlines an approach that advocates reduction in physical storage of information, an increase in housing of personnel who manage information, and a collection development policy that focuses on filling users' critical information needs rather than on building a comprehensive collection.

Impact on Professional Roles

As Internet access has spread within the library community, professionals have begun to incorporate use of the Internet into their areas of responsibility. These changes have begun to be reflected in job titles, ranging from direct service positions to upper-level administrative jobs. Titles such as "Networked Information Resources Librarian," Internet Services Coordinator," or "Electronic Resources Librarian" simply did not exist five years ago. Allen (1995) observes that libraries as organizations can adapt to technological change by creating new types of positions that eventually help to integrate the new technology into the mainstream of library operations. Unlike the earlier position of Online Search Coordinator established in the 1970s, Internet and networked resources positions cross over departmental boundaries, and they are equally likely to be found in the Reference or in the Library Systems departments, depending on the amount of technical skill required to perform the job.

An examination of 23 postings for librarian positions in a single issue of the *Chronicle of Higher Education* (September 15,1995) revealed nine position descriptions in which responsibilities that include use of Internet or networked resources is a noted component of the position. Job titles include the following:

Systems Librarian (I)
Electronic Systems Librarian (I)
Law Librarian for Internet Services (I)

Network Services Librarian (I)
Public Services/Reference Librarian (with emphasis on Internet resources (2)
Database Coordinator (I)
Network Coordinator (I)
Electronic Information Services Librarian (I)

Four of the nine positions are located in the Reference or User Services departments of their respective libraries and two report to the Director of Library Systems; the other two position descriptions do not indicate a home department. The following statements were found among the qualifications required for the nine positions:

> "Advanced work in computing and information science."
>
> "Experience with online integrated library systems, campus networks, the Internet, and electronic information resources."
>
> "Strong public service orientation, experience with searching electronic resources (online, CD-ROM, Internet), and interest in library instruction essential."
>
> "Expert knowledge of HTML and extensive experience with Web administration and operations."

Bosseau (1995) notes that the changes brought about be the availability of networked information have affected higher level administrative positions in academic settings, resulting in the creation of combined titles for managerial positions such as "University Librarian/Associate Vice President for Information Resources," with library directors being placed in charge of "an expanded set of library and other media responsibilities." Bosseau asserts that this, among other changes, reflects recognition of the library's active role in managing technology and infrastructure services that support the delivery of effective information content to users in academic settings. He characterizes the change in the library's role in the academic setting as one that has moved from the cliche phrase "the heart of the university" to a more active and critical role as the "cardiovascular system of the university."

The presence of the Internet in the professional library arena has further blurred the traditional distinctions between technical and public service responsibilities. The major distinction may now be between primarily technical development and support skills and those that are used to help provide some method of organization and access to electronic resources. As computer and networking technologies become increasingly sophisticated, and the technical knowledge threshold is lowered, staff with traditionally lower technical skills are able to connect to and navigate the Net without assistance. Concurrently, librarians who now enter the profession seeking reference and public service positions possess more computing and networking skills than those who entered the profession as few as five years ago. This combination of simplified technologies and the increased likelihood that professionals with enhanced computing skills will enter the library market has resulted in increased professional facility with the Internet and networking resources.

Along with a shift of roles within the library profession is the overlap in training and support services between library and computing enter personnel. In a recent survey of library and computing center professionals, Shiller (1994) reported more involvement by computing services staff in providing Internet access and training. However, the survey results also indicated that librarians have considerable involvement in Internet training and support. Some survey respondents reported that team training programmes were being offered through collaboration between the library and the computer center. She states that a number of respondents viewed the roles as complementary, distinguishing between "physical access," which was attributed to the computing center, and "intellectual access," which was attributed to the library.

Communication

The Net in libraries has also created the potential for change in the professional communication of librarians and other staff. This change is the result of increased opportunities for communication with individuals or collegial groups - through any number of common channels, ranging from e-mail to listserv and other interactive or asynchronous discussion groups. While the *potential* for change exists, the expansion of professional communication depends on the administrative commitment of the library to support convenient staff access to the Net and the individual's commitment to learn to use the necessary communication protocols and software (Ives, 1995). Ives includes support staff use of the Internet as an important component of how networking (electronic of non-electronic) can empower staff, and improve library service. He suggests that use of the Internet, particularly as a communi-cation and a current awareness tool, will enable libraries to accomplish more without increasing staff and other resources. He identifies several types of Internet use that should be of value to library staff in carrying out daily responsibilities:

(i) E-mail: communication - in-house, group, organization, or committee communication; obtaining evaluative information about products; sharing information about policies and procedures; "electronic mail is the most pervasive means of tapping into a large number of knowledgeable people across the expanse of the planet" (Ives,1995, page 49).

(ii) Listervs: electronic discussion groups, usually focusing on a specific topic; there are many devoted to specific library-related topics (e.g., CDROMLAN, LIBREF-L: reference, BI-L: bibliographic instruction); listservs facilitate ongoing, daily discussion about numerous issues, but they are most useful for finding a resolution to a problem when the in-house expertise is not enough.

(iii) Remote access: for free of fee, a large selection of library and information resources is accessible through the Internet, including remote online catalogs, software archives, full-text papers, and other documents, bibliographies, and numerous numeric and bibliographic databases.

(iv) Use-Net newsgroups: discussion and news groups on all topics, including libraries, that require specific software for access—usually installed by the computer center for an organization. Very useful for current awareness, they do not clutter up individual e-mail boxes as list-servs tend to.

Some library administrators harbor concerns that staff will misuse the Internet for nonwork activities, thus lowering productivity. Ives argues, however, that library admini-strators limit the growth potential of their organizations by not enabling staff to use the Internet to discover potentially useful work-related information. Perhaps the question is not whether to provide Internet access but, rather, what types of access are appropriate to enhance a staff member's knowledge of his or her area of speciality. This issue will likely resolve itself as library staff and administrators alike discover and exchange Internet resources that further enhance their work. Strictly limiting an employee's focus to what is already known to exist prevents the serendipitous discovery of equally or perhaps more useful information.

Listservs or e-conferences comprise a substantial portion of the mainstream methods of asynchronous communication among groups on the Internet. Based on a survey of fifty-seven library-related scholarly e-conferences, Kovacs et al. (1995) concluded that library and information science professionals used e-conferences to gather research and professional information for their personal use as well as for information to enhance service to library patrons. They suggest that partici-pants view the information they obtain from e-conferences similarly to the more established sources upon which they rely to find and verify information - journals, conferences, mail, and telephone contacts. Most of the respondents were librarians or paraprofessionals in academic libraries.

McClure et al. (1994) claim that libraries need to rethink the provision of information services for a networked environment. They suggest that libraries will need to change traditional assumptions about their clientele and their information seeking behaviour. They envision that networked library services will become more demand-based than they currently are, citing the point that users will gravitate to the Internet services that best meet their needs, regardless of physical location. McCombs (1994) suggests that the provision of flexible electronic access to information that often has no physical format requires that librarians, especially those in technical services areas, will need to rethink traditional attitudes toward the access and processing of information.

Holt (1993) believes that electronic networks in general can have an important role in democratizing access to library resources. His library, the St. Louis Public Library, has already established "equity sites" in such inner city locations as YMCAs, homes for the elderly, and high schools.

As Holt puts it, these:

> ...Provide access to library materials for those who have trouble getting to their public library and/or those without computers in their homes. (Page 25)

Nevertheless, for various reasons, public libraries have lagged behind academic libraries in the exploitation of the Internet resources. Speaking from a British perspective, the Library

Association (1995) has recommended that, given access to the Internet, public libraries should:

- use their skills to identify information, whether in text, image, or sound, and route it as appropriate to people in need of it;
- Provide network access points, free or charged, as appropriate, & provide opportunities for education and training in the use of the network;
- use open information systems and broadband communications to intergrate use of the network with mainstream library services;
- publish appropriate information e.g. catalogues, community information, and archives over the networks;
- apply their skills to the management of the vast amounts of information on the networks;
- as appropriate and in partnership with the academic sector, provide information from the network to students and distance learners. (Pages 548-549)
- Ways in which the Internet is being used by British public libraries are discussed by Batt (1996a).

Perhaps the best way to understand the impact of the Internet on libraries is not by speculation or through denial, but through examination. McCLure and Lopata (1996) propose a set of evaluative methods for assessing the impact of networking on the academic environment. They suggest using standard social science research methods, such as focus groups, critical incident technique, surveys, observation and site visits, as well as collecting and analyzing standard system-generated network performance and feedback statistics. Their manual contains an overview of methods and applications, as well as sample data collection forms and information about software that can be used to measure network services and their level of use. A section of the manual is devoted to online catalog measures. They pose a series of questions for each area of network use in the academic environment. The overall network and library use questions center on the network's impact on a user's ability to find information, both inside the library and within the broader campus community:

1. Has the network affected your use of electronic information resources (Faculty, student, and librarian perception)? If yes, how?
2. Has the network affected your ability to access information in the library (Faculty, student, and librarian perception)? If yes how?
3. Has the library provided public access to the network (Faculty, student, and librarian perception)?
4. Has the network affected your ability to find the information you need in the library (Faculty, student, and librarian perception)? If yes, how?
5. Has the network affected the types of services provided by the library (Faculty, student, and librarian perception)? If yes, how?
6. Has the library been involved in developing and providing access to campus information resources on the network? (Faculty, student, and librarian perception)? If yes, how?

Their work is further evidence of the Internet's impact in bringing service units like the library and the computer center closer together with instructional units in an academic environment.

Reid (1996) has described a "process model" for the increasing integration of the Internet into library services :

> The process model is divided into five phases spaning from the acquisition of Internet experience, redesign of library

processes for the networked environment to a possible revision of the organization's information management processes.

Instruction and Training

With respect to Internet instruction and orientation, librarians appear to be finding a unique and useful niche. While Internet access providers normally furnish instructions or training in how to connect, and what general types of information are available, librarians have quickly begun to fill the void of content-based-training—e.g., how to find information on a particular topic. The traditional role of bibliographic instruction has broadened to encompass Internet use as another means for gaining access to information that is available through a librarian's assistance. The recent action by the Association of College and Research Libraries (ACRL), to change the Bibliographic Instruction Section's name to simply "Instruction Section," reflects this broadened approach to instruction and training in the library profession, regardless of whether the tools are print or electronically-based.

Since the early 1990s, several Internet self-help and instructional guides have appeared. A search in the University of Illinois online catalog, in September, 1995, revealed approximately twenty books published on Internet use since late 1992, with most appearing in 1994 or later. Authors include both computer professionals and librarians. Among the "self-help" handbooks and manuals, works by Krol (1994) and Kehoe (1993) assist all types of Internet users in better understanding how to get connected to the Net and how to locate various resources. Benson (1995) provides a handbook that is tailored to the information searching activities of librarians. Jaffe (1994) provides one of the most complete training manuals that can be used for presenting Internet workshops.

Kalin and Wright (1994) describe an Internet instruction programme that exemplifies how librarians have begun to collaborate with computing professionals to offer instruction and training that helps users learn both the technical and content ends of Internet use. Other approaches, such as that of Pask and Snow (1995), advocate the integration of Internet training into overall instruction for research information retrieval, particularly in the academic setting. They point out that librarians can apply their important knowledge of subject classification to the searching of the Internet.

Learning what the Internet is, and why it ought to be used, involves the teaching of database structure, information retrieval, and critical evaluation concepts, as well as the practical aspects of getting connected. Librarians have embraced the challenging task of designing instruction that combines the teaching of skills as well as evaluative techniques. Since the early 1980s, librarians involved in instruction have found themselves training on an increasingly conceptual level about the skills needed to correctly characterize an information need and to locate relevant information, whether in print or electronic form. Perhaps one of the greatest challenges in teaching use of the Internet lies in training learners to employ "work around" techniques when they encounter common communications or other network problems. Numerous authors have commented that the two critical components of Internet training are the use of systematic search techniques and concepts, and critical evaluative skills. These skills, many suggest, are the ones that will enable Internet users to sift efficiently through the information they retrieve from disparate sources of varying degrees of validity (Pask and Snow, 1995). Connell and Franklin (1994) point out that the Internet has had a significant impact on how work and study is accomplished in academic and commercial settings. They suggest that varied approaches to instruction and training, that incorporate critical thinking and collaboration, will enable users to best locate and exploit Internet resources.

For libraries, one of the most attractive features of the Internet is its capability to support connections among remote systems. Within recent years, the library community has become increasingly involved with computer and other information professionals to create and implement standards for networking and for data sharing. Since the early 1980s, libraries have been working to implement the basic component layers of the OSI (Open Systems Interconnection) communications protocols. OSI comprises a complex see of communication protocols designed to enable different systems to communicate across a network. More recently, the ANSI Z39.50 protocol suite was developed and implemented by groups of libraries and by vendors of commercial library systems. These protocols provide guidelines and structure so that, for example, two libraries could design software that enables a user from Library to formulate a search using the familiar commands of its own online catalog, execute the search across the network on Library 2's online catalog, retrieve the result set, and display it through Library's online catalog.

A number of libraries have implemented Z39.50 in collaboration with reciprocal partners or in consortia as a means to enable users to search across different online catalog systems without having to learn the commands for the unfamiliar system. Carson and Freivalds (1993) describe one of the first such Z39.50 implementations. Numerous vendors have incorporated Z39.50 into their current OPAC systems and Z39.50 development continues, with both national and international involvement and an organized group which meets regularly to shape the content of changes and enhancements to the suite. Michael and Hinebusch (1995) provide an excellent analysis of the development of the Z39.50 protocol and its implementation in libraries.

The Internet has begun to affect the ways in which libraries describe and catalog resources. In 1994 the USMARC 856 field was established to provide for the description and retrieval of electronic materials on the Internet, and there is growing recognition of the need to develop methods for describing electronic sources that are not produced in the same manner as print publications and, therefore, not appropriate to the MARC format. A critical issue that the library community now faces is that of determining how to describe literally millions of items in their collections (photographs, pictures, manuscripts, video, and so on) for which they can never hope to provide exhaustive cataloging. While our experience with cataloging and indexing places the library community in good standing to influence the types of "metadata" standards that are employed in describing Web resources, we have difficulty incorporating new approaches to information description into the existing methods of bibliographic description and control.

Librarians and computer professionals from numerous disciplines have been working to develop sets of standards for description and access to electronic information, including full text, We-based resources, e-journals, and other resources. Current standards used to describe both print and electronic information, besides USMARC, are the TEI (Text Encoding Initiative) Header, developed by humanities computing researchers and used to describe SGML-encoded electronic texts, and the URC (Uniform Resource Citation) standard for accessing Web materials. Gaynor (1994) describes a project at the University of Virginia Library where efforts to provide bibliographic control and access through changes to traditional cataloging practices have included the use of both MARC records and TEI headers. Access to the cataloged records for electronic texts is now provided through Virginia's OPAC. This process necessitated that catalogers become familiar with the information in TEI headers. Thus, the catalogers involved in the project learned the TEI guidelines and developed a TEI header work form as well as on OCLC MARC work form (on paper) in an effort to centralize all of the available information about the electronic text to be cataloged and described. Results of the project suggested that the creation of both MARC records and TEI headers was labour-and time-intensive, with considerable duplication of work. The study recommended the purchase of better hardware and software, and also the development of an automatic SGML-MARC conversion programme to convert TEI headers in to MARC like records.

Dunsire (1995) reports on Project CATRIONA (Cataloguing and Retrieval of Information Over Networks Applications), a project to investigate the cataloging of electronic information resources and the implementation of Z39.50. The Z39.50 search and retrieve protocol is being implemented so that users of OPACs at one university can retrieve records for electronic resources from another. MARC records are used for the cataloging of e-journals, CD-ROM's and Internet resources. In principle, a range of Z39.50-based OPACs can be searched server by server, thus making feasible the implementation of a distributed catalog of Internet resources (Nocholson et al., 1995). In 1995, OCLC, along with the National Center for Supercomputing Applications (NCSA), sponsored a metadata workshop with the objective of defining a simple and usable standard for describing networked information resources (Weibel et al., 1995). Researchers at OCLC have developed an experimental system that automatically translates between MARC, TEI, and the Web-based URC. Vizine-Goetz et al. (1995) have developed the Spectrum system, which allows users to create data records in HTML (Hypertext Markup Language) format, builds a database of user-created descriptive records, and provides search and retrieval capabilities. Spectrum was built from standard Web browser components, including the Mosaic Web browser software. An interesting feature of the Spectrum system is the record creation subsystem, which processes the descriptive information input by the user and generates from it a URC (Uniform Resource Citation), TEI, or MARC record. Vizine-Goetz et al. point out that the TEI And MARC records lack required publisher data. They note that the Spectrum system will be used to create records for inclusion in OCLC's Newton database management system, which is accessible through the Mosaic Web browser software and conforms to the Z39.50 information retrieval protocol. Future plans include integrating Spectrum's functions for creating and retrieving records directly into OCLC's Web Z Server, which is currently under development.

Numerous Internet information providers are also using information organization tools, most of which provide only simple and limited subject or name access, but nevertheless are in popular use.

World Wide Web: Simplified Access to the Internet

In addition to the convenience of the Internet's global connections, the scientific community engineered the World Wide Web (Web)—a method for using graphical user interface software (now commonly referred to as *browsers*) and a form of hypertext programming language (HTML). Users of the Web can view graphical and textual information easily and legibly on the computer screen, and can move seamlessly among disparate sources and formats of information accessible from the same electronic document by means of hypertext links to files stored in various locations across the Net. Web access has popularized the Internet to an even greater extent that before.

One of the more profound developments arising from Web access is the capability for individuals to become their own Internet publishers. Any individual with an Internet connection and a computer can occupy space on the Web. The Web has thus brought about the establishment of many commercial, not-for-profit, and private communication and publishing activities on the Internet.

Weibel (1995a,b) provides an excellent description of Web structure and services that can be offered through the Web, including publishing. He also reviewed the access and organization tools developed for use on the Web, but developments are occurring so rapidly that his review is already rather out of date.

Commercial bibliographic vendors, including OCLC, have begun to migrate their text-based Internet services to a Web environment. The OCLC First Search system, which provides access to over 55 bibliographic databases, is available through various Web browsers. The search functionality is identical to the text-based First Search database, which supports features such as worldlists, Boolean operators, and search limits. There is a need for further development of tools that provide consistent and organized access to the disparate resource types on the Internet. An entity called the Internet Engineering Task Force (IETF) was established in the early 1990s to address the formation of conventions that enable the development of these tools. Membership on the IETF includes computer professionals, scientists, and more recently, librarians, with OCLC maintaining an active representative role. While many Web searching engines have appeared, the depth of indexing is limited, with few powerful search filters in operation.

Until recently, the Web suffered from the searching condition known as "statelessness." Once a search is executed and the information from a hyperlink is delivered, the connection to the link is broken, precluding further refinement of the user's search query. Being able to build a subsequent search on the results of a previously retrieved set, as common in many searching systems, makes the Web a model closer to that which we now find familiar with library online resources. Ongoing development work on software called Common Gateway Interface (CGI) is helping to resolve the stateless Web issue in the near term, and makes it possible for the introduction of well-defined classification and searching tools that cut across the Web. CGI programming makes it possible for users to submit powerful database queries from Web browsers. Several Web-based search engines now employ CGI programming in this manner. Further programming developments, such as the creation of Sun Microsystems Java language, now enable the delivery of "applets" or bits of programmes across the network to provide animation, audio, video, and three-dimensional displays, all available through the Web (Gordon, 1996). The impact of these technologies on knowledge management, and on the concept of document structure and content, is considerable. For example, a Web "document" can consist of text, images, audio, and video. The various media that comprise a Web document can come from local, remote, or a combination of network locations.

The shape or content of that document can be changed at any time, depending on the interests of its author, or the content of its hypermedia links. OCLC has devoted considerable research effort to the development of retrieval services on the Internet that allow for the continual verification of electronic resources. One such service, Netfirst, identifies, catalogs, and continually verifies the existence and location of Web information resources. OCLC is also sponsoring the Internet database, an effort to create a shared database of cataloging records for Internet-accessible e-journals and other electronic resources, and has contributed to research efforts to establish standards for encoding and accessing electronic resources.

While a vast amount of literature has already appeared on the subject of libraries and the Internet, surprisingly little of this is at the broadest management level —e.g., how Internet implementation and use in libraries should be managed or, conversely, how net use affects management practices in libraries. This is in contrast with the Internet literature dealing with business, government, and academic in general where such broad issues are frequently discussed. It is legitimate, of course, to ask if the Internet has been oversold as an information access tool, since each technological development introduced into libraries since the 1960s has come with exaggerated claims for labour-saving and work-revolutionizing impact. Many Internet problems exist. Network communication problems are often encountered by Internet users regardless for their expertise in searching. Retrieval problems are common, due to lack of standardization and poor organization, and some Internet search engines cannot provide the depth of retrieval that is currently offered by many OPACs. Moreover, the rapidly increasing volume of use is creating significant degradation of performance and response time in some cases. All these weaknesses notwithstanding, the rapid assimilation of the Internet into all aspects of library activities suggests that it will continue to develop as an important information resource and means of communication among libraries and their users.

E-BOOK

As a recent development, an e-book is the digital media equivalent of a conventional printed book. Such documents are usually read on personal computers, or on dedicated hardware devices known as *e-book readers* or *e-book devices*. Many mobile phones can also be used to read eBooks. Early e-books were generally written for specialty areas and a limited audience, meant to be read only by small and devoted interest groups. The scope of the subject matter of these e-books included technical manuals for hardware, manufacturing techniques, and other subjects. Numerous e-book formats emerged and proliferated, some supported by major software companies such as Adobe's PDF format, and others supported by independent and open-source programmers.

Multiple readers naturally followed multiple formats, most of them specializing in only one format, and thereby fragmenting the e-book market even more. Due to exclusiveness and limited readerships of e-books, the fractured market of independents and specialty authors lacked consensus regarding a standard for packaging and selling e-books. E-books continued to gain in their own underground markets. Many e-book publishers began distributing books that were in the public domain. At the same time, authors with books that were not accepted by publishers offered their works online so they could be seen by others. Unofficial (and occasionally unauthorized) catalogs of books became available over the web, and sites devoted to e-books began disseminating information about e-books to the public. As of 2008, new marketing models for e-books were being developed and dedicated reading hardware was produced. E-books (as opposed to ebook readers) have probably already achieved global distribution thanks to the Internet. Actual details are unquantified or unqualified - but of course anyone with a computer can read an ebook - you don't need an ebook reader.

Only two e-book readers dominate the market, Amazon's Kindle model or Sony's PRS-500. E-books have seen good growth in Japan throughout the 2000s and it currently has an e-book market worth ¥10 billion. However, not all authors have endorsed the concept of electronic publishing. J.K Rowling, author of the Harry Potter series, has stated that there will be no e-versions of the books. Experts from Plastic Logic, a display technology company based in Cambridge, UK, reported of a technique that allows printing polymer transistors onto a surface of flexible plastic. This technique makes it possible for the screens to bend and bounce, thus giving the e-books additional endurance.

Comparison of E-books with Printed Books

Advantages

(a) Text can be searched automatically and cross-referenced using hyperlinks.

(b) A single e-book reader containing several books is easier to carry around (less mass and volume) than the same books in printed form. Even hundreds or thousands of books may be stored on the same device.

(c) E-books can allow non-permanent highlighting and annotation.

(d) Although they require electricity to be read, the production of e-books does not consume the paper, ink, and other resources that are used to produce printed books.

(e) Font size and font face can be adjusted.

(f) E-books may allow animated images or multimedia clips to be embedded.

(g) E-books allow for greater fidelity in colour reproduction compared to CMYK colour printing (although some e-book readers have only monochrome displays).

(h) E-book devices allow reading in low light or even total darkness by means of a back light.

(i) An e-book can automatically open at the last read page.

(j) While an e-book reader costs more than one book, the electronic texts are generally cheaper.

(k) Also for the supplier e-books require little space, they can therefore be offered indefinitely, with no going out of print date, allowing authors to continue to earn royalties indefinitely.

(l) Text-to-speech software can be used to convert e-books to audio books automatically.

(m) Ease of distributing e-texts means that they can be used to stimulate higher sales of printed copies of books.

(n) It is easier for authors to self-publish e-books.

Problems

(a) E-book readers are more fragile than paper books and more susceptible to physical damage.

(b) A small book is easier to carry around (less mass and volume) than an e-book.

(c) If not viewed on computers, e-books require the purchase of an electronic device and/or peripheral software which can display them. If they are to be viewed on a personal computer, it may require additional software

(d) Most publishers don't produce the e-book equivalent of their printed books. In other cases, e-books are given a lower priority in terms of the publisher's resources, resulting in a disparity in product quality, release dates and the like. This problem is not endemic to every publisher, but has an effect on the quality of the overall pool of merchandise available.

(e) E-book readers are more likely to be stolen than paper books.

(f) Looking at a screen for a long time may cause eye strain and sometimes headaches.

(g) E-book readers can malfunction due to faults in hardware or software, such as hard disk drive failure.

(h) E-book readers require electrical power; in the case of mobile use, the battery can get exhausted.

(i) E-books can be easily hacked through the use of hardware or software modifications and widely disseminated on the Internet and/or other e-book readers, without approval from the author or publisher.

(j) If an e-book device is stolen, lost, or broken beyond repair, all e-books stored on the device may be lost. This can be avoided by backup either on another device or by the e-book provider.

(k) Screen resolution of reading devices may be lower than actual paper, making it difficult to read e-books.

(l) From the reader's perspective, conventional ownership, fair use, and access to the book's content is challenged and restricted by Digital Rights Management.

(m) There is a loss of tactility and aesthetics of book-bindings. Also lost is the ability to very quickly riffle through the pages to search for a particular section or to get a sense of the book merely by sight.

(n) While the written language is universal for books, e-books are deliberatly prevented from downloading certain formats, meaning the owner has to buy a different model for each format.

The greatest disadvantage in an e-book is piracy. Most proprietary software were termed secure but soon pirated copies flooded the underground market. The same could be said of the e-book as well. Books are much more difficult to duplicate in an amateur printing press.

Digital Rights Management

Anti-circumvention techniques may be used to restrict what the user may do with an e-book. For instance, it may not be possible to transfer ownership of an e-book to another person, though such a transaction is common with physical books. Some devices can phone home to track readers and reading habits, restrict printing, or arbitrarily modify reading material. This includes restricting the copying and distribution of works in the public domain through the use of "click-wrap" licensing, effectively limiting the rights of the public to distribute, sell or use texts in the public domain freely.

Most e-book publishers do not warn their customers about the possible implications of the digital rights management tied to their products. Generally they claim that digital rights management is meant to prevent copying of the e-book. However in many cases it is also possible that digital rights management will result in the complete denial of access by the purchaser to the e-book.

With some formats of DRM, the e-book is tied to a specific computer or device. In these cases the DRM will usually let the purchaser move the book a limited number of times after which he cannot use it on any additional devices. If the purchaser upgrades or replaces their devices eventually they may lose access to their purchase. Some forms of digital rights management depend on the existence of online services to authenticate the purchasers. When the company that provides the service goes out of business or decides to stop providing the service, the purchaser will no longer be able to access the e-book. With digital rights management, it is argued by some to be a more apt use of money for commodity to be a rental or lease rather than a purchase. The restricted book comes with a number of restrictions, and eventually access to the purchase can be removed by a number of different parties involved. These include the publisher of the book, the publisher of the DRM scheme, and the publisher of the reader software. These are all things that are significantly different from the realm of experiences anyone has had with a physical copy of the book.

Some e-books are produced simultaneously with the production of a printed format, as described in electronic publishing, though in many instances they may not be put on sale until later. Often, e-books are produced from pre-existing hard-copy books, generally by document scanning, sometimes with the use of robotic book scanners, having the technology to quickly scan books without damaging the original print edition. Scanning a book produces an image file, which must then be converted into text format by an OCR programme. Occasionally, as in some e-text projects, a book may be produced by re-entering the text from a keyboard. As a newer development, sometimes only the electronic version of a book is produced by the publisher. It is also possible to convert electronic book to a printed book by print on demand.

However this an exception as tradition dictates that a book be launched in the print format and later if the author wishes, an electronic version is also produced. Among the first Internet-only publishers of new e-books were Boson Books, Hard Shell Word Factory and Online Originals, all founded in the mid-1990s. Each pioneered different aspects of what has since become common practice amongst e-book publishers, e.g. the support of multiple formats including PDFs, the payment of much higher royalty rates than conventional publishers, and the online presentation of free samples. Hard Shell Word Factory set the first professional standards for commercial e-books and pioneered author-friendly contracts. Online Originals was the first e-book publisher to win mainstream book reviews (in The Times) and a nomination for a major literary prize (the Booker Prize). In 2004-2005, many newcomers to e-book publishing have included major print publishers. At the same time, e-publishers have started to offer print versions of many of their titles. Thus the line between the two is fast blurring.

There are some parts of the industry where there are particularly notable leading firms. In the general field of science-fiction and fantasy, Baen Books, an American publishing company established in 1983 by science fiction publishing industry long-timer Jim Baen (1943-2006) has a well-established position. It is a science fiction and fantasy publishing house that specializes in space opera/military science fiction and fantasy (though it does not restrict itself to these subgenres).

It is notable for releasing books without DRM in a variety of formats, before hard-copy publication, and pre-releasing ebooks in parts before the hard-copy release. Many older titles are available for free, especially the first book in a series. E-books have their own bestseller lists, including those compiled by

IDPF, BooksOnBoard and Fictionwise. There are two yearly awards for excellence in e-books. The longest-standing and most inclusive of these is the EPPIE award, given by EPIC since 2000. The other is the Dream Realm Award, first awarded to speculative fiction e-books in 2002.

Readers

E-book readers may be specifically designed for that purpose, or intended for other purposes as well. The term is restricted to hardware devices, not software programmes. Specialized devices have the advantage of doing one thing well. Specifically, they tend to have the right screen size, battery lifespan, lighting and weight. A disadvantage of such devices is that they are often expensive when compared to generic devices such as laptops and PDAs.

Some prominent examples include:

- Pixelar e-Reader by Pixelar (2008/9)
- Plastic Logic (2009 estimate)
- Kindle by Amazon (2007)
- Kindle 2 by Amazon (2009)
- Cybook Gen3 by Bookeen (2007)
- Hanlin eReader by Jinke (distributed as "Lbook" in Estonia, Kazakhstan, Russia and Ukraine as "BeBook" in Europe) (2007)
- Sony Reader by Sony (2006)
- Liad by iRex (2006)
- Librié by Sony (2004)

E-BOOK FORMATS COMPARISON

The following is a comparison of e-book formats used to create and publish e-books. A writer or publisher has many options when it comes to choosing a format for production. While the average end-user might arguably simply want to read books, every format has its proponents and champions, and debates over "which format is best" can become intense. The myriad of e-book formats is sometimes referred to as the "Tower of eBabel". For the average end user to read a book, every format has its advantages and disadvantages. Formats available include, but are by no means limited to:

Open Electronic Book Package Format

OPF is an XML-based e-book format created by E-Book Systems.

Hypertext Markup Language

HTML is the markup language used for most web pages. E-books using HTML can be read using a Web browser. The specifications to the format are freely available from the W3C.

As markup language, HTML adds especially marked meta elements to otherwise plain text encoded using character sets like ASCII or UTF-8. As such suitably formatted files can be, and sometimes are, generated *by hand* using a *plain text editor* or *programmer's editor*. Many *HTML generator* applications exist to ease this process and often require less intricate knowledge of the format details involved.

HTML is not a particularly efficient format to store information, requiring more storage space for a given work than many other formats, even if images are not used to illustrate it. The format does not describe pages and has no facility to store multiple things (images, etc.) in a single file. Often e-books in this format will store one chapter per file.

Plain Text Files

E-books in plain text exist and are very small in size. For example, the bible is about 4 MB.

Amazon Kindle (AZW) Format

With the launch of the Kindle eBook reader, Amazon.com created the AZW format. It is based on the Mobipocket standard, with a slightly different serial number scheme (it uses an asterisk instead of a Dollar sign) and its own DRM formatting. Because the eBooks bought on the Kindle are delivered wirelessly over EvDO (the system is called Whispernet by Amazon), the user does not see the AZW files during the download process.

TomeRaider

The TomeRaider e-book format is a proprietary format. There are versions of TomeRaider for Windows, Windows Mobile (aka Pocket PC), Palm, Symbian and more. Several Wikipedias are available as TomeRaider files with all articles unabridged, some even with nearly all images. Capabilities of the TomeRaider3 ebook reader vary considerably per platform: the Windows and Windows Mobile editions support full HTML and CSS. The Palm edition supports limited HTML (e.g. no tables, no fonts), and CSS support is missing. For Symbian there is only the older TomeRaider2 format, which does not render images or offer category search facilities. Despite these differences any TomeRaider ebook can be browsed on all platforms. Tomeraider is popular among readers because of its huge free document base. According to their records the Tomeraider Website has over 4000 free ebooks to read. The IMDB movie database is also as a regularly updated Tomeraider ebook. Tomeraider developers have recently developed full Wikipedia (English version up to 2007 December data) as an ebook, which is 3.3GB file. You can download the file here with payment for bandwidth, but free for 2006 October data which is 1GB file.

NISO Z39.86 Format

DAISY is an XML-based e-book format created by the DAISY international consortium of libraries for people with print disabilities.

DAISY implementations have focused on two main types: audio e-books and text e-books. A subset of the DAISY format has been adopted by law in the United States as the National Instructional Material Accessibility Standard, and K-12 textbooks and instructional materials are now required to be provided to students with disabilities.

Arghos Diffusion

The ARG format is an XML-based proprietary format developed by the French firm Arghos Diffusion.

ARG files use a proprietary DRM and encryption method and are readable only in the *Arghos Player*.

It supports various input formats for text, audio or video, such as PDF, WMA, MP3, WMV, and allows multiple interactive functions such as bookmarking, advanced plain-text searching, dynamic text highlighting, etc.

Flip Books

A "Flip Book" is a type of E-Book distinguished by virtual pages that actually "flip", much like turning pages of paper in a real book or magazine. The first dynamic Flip Book Reader was developed in 2003/2004 by Interaxive Media for Nishe Media (Canada) and was therefore called "Nishe Pages". The first version was produced in part by Cybaris (Canada) and was first publicly showcased in August 2004. Soon thereafter, many copycat "flip books" started appearing thanks to technological advances in Macromedia Flash, mostly hardcoded using Flash components. The original software remains unique in that it is powered by a complete server-based CMS system that allows the books to be created, published, and viewed remotely from a web server without requiring any custom software to be installed. Nishe Media went defunct in 2004, leaving the unfinished software to Interaxive Media who continued its development in Hong Kong. Though not widely used outside of Asia, it is now at version 3.0 and is arguably the most advanced server-based E-Book platform. It remains privately held by the original developer, Ryan Sutherland, owner and founder of Interaxive Media.

FictionBook

FictionBook is a popular XML-based e-book format, supported by free readers such as Haali Reader and FBReader.

Text Encoding Initiative

TEI Lite is the most popular of the TEI-based (and thus XML-based or SGML-based) electronic text formats.

Plucker

Plucker is a free e-book reader application with its own associated file format and software to automatically generate plucker files from HTML files, web sites or RSS feeds. The format is a compressed HTML archive, somewhat like Microsoft's CHM.

CHM Format

CHM format is a proprietary format based on HTML. Multiple pages and embedded graphics are distributed along with proprietary metadata as a single compressed file. In contrast, in HTML, a site consists of multiple HTML files and associated image files in standardized formats.

Portable Document Format (PDF)

A file format created by Adobe Systems, initially to provide a standard form for storing and editing printed publishable documents. The format derives from PostScript by removing language features like loops and adding support for things like compression and passwords. Because PDF documents can easily be viewed and printed by users on a variety of computer platforms, they are very common on the World Wide Web. The specification of the format is freely available from Adobe.

PDF files typically contain brochures, product manuals, magazine articles, up to entire books, as they can embed fonts, images, and other documents. A PDF file contains one or more page images, each of which you can zoom in on or out from. Since the format is designed to reproduce page images, the text cannot be re-flowed to fit the screen width, PDF files designed for printing on standard paper sizes are less easily viewed on screens with limited size or resolution such as found on mobile phones and PDAs.

Adobe has addressed this by adding a re-flow facility to its Acrobat Reader software, but for this to work the document must be marked for re-flowing at creation, which means existing PDF documents will not benefit. The Windows Mobile (aka Pocket PC) version of Adobe Acrobat will automatically attempt to tag a PDF for reflow during the synchronization process. This tagging process will not work on most locked PDF documents. When using Windows Vista with a Windows Mobile device and Adobe Acrobat, this tagging process must occur before the device is synchronized. Multiple Adobe products support creating PDF files, such as Adobe Acrobat and Acrobat Capture, as do third-party products such as PDFCreator, OpenOffice.org, and FOP, and several programming libraries. Acrobat Reader (now simply called *Adobe Reader*) is Adobe's product used to view PDF files, with third party viewers such as xpdf also available.

Later versions of the specification add support for forms, comments, hypertext links, and even interactive elements such as buttons for forms entry and for triggering sound and video. Such features may not be supported by older or third-party viewers and some are not transferrable to print.

Microsoft LIT

DRM-protected LIT files are only readable in the proprietary Microsoft Reader programme, as the .LIT format, otherwise similar to Microsoft's CHM format, includes Digital Rights Management features. Other third party readers, such as Lexcycle Stanza, can read unprotected LIT files. There are also tools such as Convert Lit, which can convert .lit files to HTML files or OEBPS files.

The MS reader uses patented ClearType display technology. In Reader navigation works with a keyboard, mouse, stylus, or through electronic bookmarks. The Catalogue Library records reader books in a personalized "home page", and books are displayed with ClearType to improve readability. A user can add annotations and notes to any page, create large-print e-books with a single command, or create free-form drawings on the reader pages. A built-in dictionary allows the user to look up words.

DjVu

DjVu is a format that specialises in and particularly excels at storing scanned images. It includes advanced compressors optimized for low-color images, such as text documents. Individual files may contain one or more pages.

The format has long remained in obscurity, but now that free tools to manipulate the format are available, that is starting to change. The contained page images are divided in separate layers (such as multi-color, low-resolution, lossily-compressed background layer, and few-colors, high-resolution, tightly-compressed foreground layer), each compressed in the best available method. The format is designed to decompress very quickly, even faster than vector-based formats. The advantage of DjVu is that it is possible to take a high-resolution scan (300-400 DPI), good enough for both on-screen reading and printing, and store it very efficiently. Several dozens of 300 DPI black-and-white scans can be stored in less than a megabyte.

PostScript

PostScript is a page description language used in the electronic and desktop publishing areas for describing the contents of a printed page in a higher level than the actual output bitmap. Many office printers directly support interpreting PostScript and printing the result. As a result of that, the format also sees wide use in the Unix world.

eReader

eReader is a freeware programme for viewing Palm Digital Media electronic books. Versions are available for PalmOS, iPhone, Symbian, Windows Mobile Pocket PC/Smartphone, desktop Windows, and Macintosh. The reader shows text one page at a time as paper books do. eReader supports embedded hyperlinks and images. Additionally the Stanza application for the iPhone and iPod Touch can read both encrypted and unencrypted eReader files.

The company's web site - ereader.com offers a wide selection of eReader-formatted ebooks available for purchase and download, and also a few for free. The paid-for books are encrypted, with the key being the purchaser's full name and credit card number. This information is not stored in the ebook though. A one-way hash is used, so there no risk of the user's information being extracted. The programme supports features like bookmarks and footnotes, enabling the user to mark any page with a bookmark, and any part of the text with a footnote-like commentary. Footnotes can later be exported as a Memo document.

The company also offers two Windows/MacOS programmes for producing ebooks: the free Dropbook, and the paid-for eBook Studio. Dropbook is simply a file-oriented PML-to-PDB converter, and eBook Studio incorporates a WYSIWYG editor. PML (Palm Markup Language) is basically text with embedded formatting tags, so feeding a pure text file into eBook Studio or Dropbook also works.

There is also support for an integrated reference dictionary (with many options up to and including a 476,000-word Merrian-Webster Dictionary, including pronunciation keys) so that any word in the text can be highlighted and looked up on the dictionary instantly. Commercial fonts can also be individually purchased and downloaded at the company's web site, ereader.com.

Desktop Author

Desktop Author is an electronic publishing suite that allows creation of digital web books with virtual turning pages. Digital web books of any publication type can be written in this format, including brochures, e-books, digital photo albums, e-cards, digital diaries, online resumes, quizzes, exams, tests, forms and surveys. DesktopAuthor packages the e-book into a ".dnl" or ".exe" book. Each can be a single, plain stand-alone executable file which does not require any other programmes to view it. DNL files can be viewed inside a web browser or stand-alone via the **DNL Reader**.

DNL Reader

DNL format is an e-Book format, one which replicates the real life alternative, namely page turning Books. The DNL e-Book is developed by [DNAML Pty Limited] an Australian company established in 1999. THE DNL e-Book can be produced using DeskTop Author or DeskTop Communicator.

Newton eBook

Commonly known as an Apple Newton book; a single Newton package file can contain multiple books (for example, the three books of a trilogy might be packaged together).

All systems running the Newton operating system (the most

common include the Newton MessagePads, eMates, Siemens Secretary Stations, Motorola Marcos, Digital Ocean Seahorses and Tarpons) have built-in support for viewing Newton books. The Newton package format was released to the public by Newton, Inc. prior to that company's absorption into Apple Computer. The format is thus arguably open and various people have written readers for it (writing a Newton book converter has even been assigned as a university-level class project).

Newton books have no support for DRM or encryption. They do support internal links, potentially multiple tables of contents and indexes, embedded grayscale images, and even some scripting capability (for example, it's possible to make a book in which the reader can influence the outcome).

Newton books utilize Unicode and are thus available in numerous languages. An individual Newton book may actually contain multiple views representing the same content in different ways (such as for different screen resolutions).

APABI

APABI is a format deviced by Founder Electronics. It is a popular format for Chinese e-books. It can be read using the Apabi Reader software, and produced using Apabi Publisher. Both .xeb and .ceb files are encoded binary files. The Iliad e-book device includes an Apabi 'viewer'.

iPod Notes

Notes is a feature of iPod that allows short text notes to be displayed on the iPod screen. As the size limit for one note is 4096 bytes, there are some tools that create the notes from the longer plain text file. Basic HTML is allowed, but otherwise the format is plain text only.

Libris

Libris is a Java based eBook reader for mobile devices such

as cell phones. Libris will run on most Java enabled devices that support MIDP. The reader formats books to fit the device screen, and shows one page at a time using high quality anti-aliased fonts. Books may employ encryption or be unrestricted. Libris content may be produced using the MakeLibris tool. The Libris reader also supports the PalmDoc format.

Mobipocket

The Mobipocket e-book format based on the Open eBook standard using XHTML can include JavaScript and frames. It also supports native SQL queries to be used with embedded databases. There is a corresponding e-book reader. A free e-book of the German Wikipedia has been published in Mobipocket format .

The Mobipocket Reader has a home page library. Readers can add blank pages in any part of a book and add free-hand drawings. Annotations — highlights, bookmarks, corrections, notes, and drawings — can be applied, organized, and recalled from a single location. Mobipocket Reader has electronic bookmarks, and a built-in dictionary

The reader has a full screen mode for reading and support for many PDAs, Communicators, and Smartphones. Mobipocket products support most Windows, Symbian, BlackBerry and Palm operating systems, but not Linux or Macintosh.

IDPF/EPUB

The .epub or OEBPS format is an open standard for eBooks created by the International Digital Publishing Forum (IDPF). It combines three IDPF open standards:

- Open Publication Structure (OPS) 2.0, which describes the content markup (either XHTML or Daisy DTBook)
- Open Packaging Format (OPF) 2.0, which describes the structure of an .epub in XML

- OEBPS Container Format (OCF) 1.0, which bundles files together (as a renamed ZIP file)

Currently, the format can be read by Adobe Digital Editions, Lexcycle Stanza, BookGlutton and the Mozilla Firefox plugin OpenBerg Lector. Several other reader software programmes are currently implementing support for the format, such as dotReader, FBReader, Mobipocket and Okular. Another software .epub reader, Lucidor, is in beta. As of 7/23/2008, an update to the Sony Reader will allow the device to read .epub documents. In 2008 BookGlutton released a free HTML-to-EPUB converter.

SSReader

The digital book format used by a popular digital library company in China. It is a proprietary raster image compression and binding format, with reading time OCR plugin modules. The company scanned a huge number of Chinese books in the China National Library and this becomes the major stock of their service. The detailed format is not published. There are also some other commercial ebook formats used in Chinese digital libraries.

Multimedia Books (Eveda)

A Multimedia EBook is media and book content that utilizes a combination of different book content forms. The term can be used as a noun (a medium with multiple content forms) or as an adjective describing a medium as having multiple content forms. The term is used in contrast to media which only utilize traditional forms of printed or text book.

Multimedia EBook includes a combination of text, audio, still images, animation, video, and interactivity content forms. Multimedia EBook used for creation on the basis of a literary fiction book, addition of the audio-visual and interactive contents, the new form of creativity. The user (the former reader) has an opportunity to participate in events occuring to characters, to feel influence of a musical part of a narration and graphic part. The perception of several media forms of contents considerably expands depth of transfer power of art and creativity.

E-BOOK READER MATRIX

Much of the renewed enthusiasm for e-books comes from a new generation of e-book reader devices because they use the E Ink technology which has been eagerly awaited, and the feature sets are much richer than devices could offer in the past. This new display technology has the distinct advantage of using power for page turns only, not to maintain a page display. But most importantly, it provides a crisp, clear image on a larger display screen that rivals print seen in paper books.

If you were really looking for a more generalized solution check Mobile devices.

Devices

The main manufactures of eBook dedicated device hardware are: Sony, Jinke, Netronix, Amazon and IRex. However, some devices are branded with different names. These devices may be exactly the same as the 5 mentioned above or may have different firmware and therefore some significantly different specifications in that area.

Sony Portable Reader is the generic name for several Sony devices. Jinke Electronics creates the Hanlin eBook V3 and several other models. These products are branded under several different names including IBook, BeBook and Astak EZ Reader. The Amazon Kindle is only sold by Amazon. The Netronix brand is generally not seen in an end user product. Instead you will see devices such as the STAReBOOK and the Bookeen Cybook Gen3 that have the same basic hardware, the Netronix

EB-600, but different firmware. Other Netronix devices include the NUUT, Soribook, and ESlick.

The "high-end" devices are currently supported by the iRex Digital Reader and iRex iLiad. Both Jinke Electronics and Netronix have pre-announced several new models including the eBook V9 with 9.7" display and EB-900.

There are also some new players: The Polymer Vision Readius is WinCE-based, and it is cell phone sized with a rollup QVGA screen. The Plastic Logic devices will give iRex some competition.

ELECTRONIC JOURNAL

Basically, Electronic journals are scholarly journals or magazines that can be accessed via electronic transmission. They are a specialized form of electronic document: they have the purpose of providing material for academic research and study, they are formatted approximately like printed journal articles, the metadata is entered into specialized databases, such as DOAJ or OACI as well as the databases for the discipline, and they are predominantly available through academic libraries and special libraries. Some electronic journals are online-only journals; some are online versions of printed journals, and some consist of the online equivalent of a printed journal, but with additional online-only material.

Remarkably, commercial sites are subscription-based, or allow pay-per-view access. Many universities subscribe to electronic journals to provide access to their students and faculty, and it is generally also possible for individuals to subscribe. An increasing number of journals are now available as open access journals, requiring no subscription. Most working paper archives and articles on personal homepages are free, as are collections in institutional repositories and subject repositories.

Most electronic journals are published both in HTML and PDF formats, but some are available in only one of the two. Some early electronic journals were first published in ASCII text, and some informally published ones continue in that format.

6

Computer-Based Acquisitions System and Relevant Issues

As we all know computers have revolutionised all aspects of library and information science. We shall now discuss a case study of an operational computer-based acquisitions system that applied the major principles and aspects of designing. Here we intended to illustrate the characteristics of the computer system used as well as the input/output media involved in satisfying the system's requirements.

Salient Features of the Computer System

The capabilities and limitations of computer system available to the library must be known prior to deigning the computer-based library system. In the case of the described acquisitions system the equipment available to the library was in International Business Machine System 360/50 computer installation consisting of the following devices listed with their IBM type number and related capabilities.

1. There were two 1403 line printers for printed output. Each printer is rated at 600 lines per minute with 132 characters per line using a printing chain with the Standard Character Set of 48 graphics (26 upper case alpha, 10 numeric, and 12 assorted special characters). Using the Full Character Set (Text Printing) chain, which includes

upper and lower case letters, numerals, and many more special characters than the Standard Set, printing speed is reduced by more than 50 per cent to about 250 lines per minute.

2. There was a 2050 central processing unit (CPU) with type 1052 typewriter and console that could handle compilation and execution of programmes together. CPU core storage is 131,172 bytes (characters)., Two 16-digit decimals may be multiplied together in 37.25 microsecond. This speed of data handling is illustrated by the fact that 18 three-line bibliographic records (call number, author, and title) plus a page heading may be formatted for printing in less than 1 second including an edit (Verification) of the call number and allowance for spaces between entries.
3. A 2540 card reader punch was available for reading punched-card input and punching output data. This machine reads 1000 cards per minute and punches 300 cards per minute.
4. There were four 2311 disk drives that house "compilers" and the various monitor systems." Compilers are programmes that translate instructions in specific programmes into the language that the machine can use. Monitor systems coordinate and direct the computer system's capabilities for maximum effectiveness in processing user programmes. There are 7.25 million characters of random (direct) access storage available from each disk drive and it may be read at 56,000 characters per second. Direct access is essential to such operations as sorting or putting a file in some desired order. For example, 3000 variable-length records can be alphabetized in less than 3 minutes including the time it takes for the input and output magnetic tapes to be rewound.

5. Five 2400 model 1 magnetic tape drives for general input/output (I/O) operations were avai-lable. There are 23 million characters of sequential storage available per tape drive deliverable at 30,000 characters per second. The tapes are useful or files that will be used but not rearranged in processing.
6. A 2671 paper-tape reader was provided. With the feed and take-up spools, paper tape is read at 1000 characters (about three book orders) per second. The spooling accessory allows tapes to be read in proper data sequence without respect to how the paper tape is wound.
7. A 2361 bulk core storage provided over one million bytes of core storage supplementing the storage capacity available in the central processing unit.
8. Peripheral utility type equipment was also available including the 129 keypunch, the burster for breaking apart paper printout, the decollator for pulling out carbon paper and separating multiple copies of a printout, the punched-card duplicating machine, and the punched-card sorter.
9. A 2841 control unit for the disk 2311 drives and a 2821 control unit for the 1403 printers and the 2540 reader were available to synchronize the I/O devices with the CPU so that the programme processing would continue during the I/O operations. Being mechanical, these operations are considerably slower than the electronic operations of the CPU.

As a prerequisite, when the decision to purchase a book was made, the analyst could see the effect this would have on the acquisition system as well as others. He applied the principle of economy of recording information only once and began the design that could satisfy this principle. He also kept in mind five major internal requirements that the new acquisitions system had to satisfy: a current on-order file, a claiming procedure, a notification to requestor, various fiscal reports, and operating statistics. In order to satisfy the system need for records in two forms, eye legible and machine readable, an input device was needed to create the records in these formats.

The key punch, although it produces punched cards that are eye legible and machine readable, was unacceptable because it could not prepare the needed multiple-copy order sets. On the other hand the paper type that serves as input to the computer. The advantage of the tape typewriter over the key punch in this ordering application appear to be : (i) the production of a conventional, typed record that facilitates the revision and making of corrections, and (ii) the familiarity of the typewriter as a tool to all library clerical personnel.

The tape typewriter used in this application is controlled by a master tape that performs the following functions:

1. Positions the order form and controls the horizontal and vertical positioning of data.
2. Maintains control over format of data to be entered. For example, if in a certain area it is required that four characters of information be inserted into the record and if the operator only centers three characters of information, the machine will stop and not continue until the field has been filled.
3. The control tape automatically inserts into the input tape the necessary control characters to identify the beginning and end of each variable-length field.

In fact, satisfaction of the requirements resulted first in a multipart book order form that was designed to fulfill the existing requirements as well as to provide the necessary input for computer processing. The function of typing the book-order set and the disposition of the output in terms of external and internal requirements.

Parts one, two, and three of the multipart form may be considered as satisfying external requirements; copy 1 to be used for the vendor's records; copy 2 to go to the vendor for return with the book or for use as a report on the book's availability; and copy 3 to be used for ordering Library of Congress catalogue cards and on return, as notification to the individual requestor of the book's availability. The paper tape provides the input for various other requirements satisfied by computer-produced reports.

1. *Current On-order File.* Under manual procedures continuous control and updating of such a file is nearly impossible. However, it is possible to update the file keep it current with the computer-based system. Further, the computer-produced on-order file reduces the manual filing operation to the maintenance of a weekly interim in-process file. The computer-produced in-process list provides a biweekly cumulated list of orders including any changes made after the original typing of the order.

2. *Claiming Procedure (order follow-up)* : Because the conditions under which a claim was initiated had to be specified in detail, this requirement cold be well satisfied by a computer-based record.

3. *Operating Statistics.* As the volume of book orders increased the task of keeping statistics obviously became more complex. The requirement of maintaining a variety of routine statistical reports and producing special reports as needed was suited to a computer control.

4. *Fiscal Reports.* In order to keep an accurate and current account of the encumbrances and expenditures of the acquisitions, system, a variety of fiscal reports were required. As the record-

keeping function increased in volume and complexity the more amenable it became to computer-based manipulation. One of the fiscal reports includes statements of funds added, withdrawn, expenditures year to date, encumbered funds, and previous and current balances for each account.

Computer Processing Storage and Output Media

Basically, it was established that the initial computer input was to be the punched-paper tape produced by the tape typewriter and that the records were then to be stored on magnetic tape for processing by the computer. The design of the machine-readable record and the system for processing it had to be developed within the framework of these two parameters, paper tape for input and magnetic tape for processing and storage. In designing the machine record and specifying the processing the first step was translation of the record from the punched-paper tape into the magnetic-tape code, which is a character-by-character translation. Here advantage was taken of the computer's abilities to structure in a predetermined format, a magnetic-tape record that makes provision for all essential data elements whether or not they are present in the record being translated.

It the translated magnetic-tape record was to be readily updated throughout, if each new record could contain any or all of the allowable data elements, and if records could be entered in random order, additional parameters had to be considered to further develop the system. As a result, two major programmes were developed: the translation programme, including formatting and editing of the record, and a general processing programme. The two programmes had to be separated by another programme because of two other seemingly incompatible requirements: that records be readily updated and that they bee accepted in random order.

To update a record it first had to be found in the file.

Finding it required that it be uniquely identifiable and implied, with sequential access storage (magnetic tape), that the records were in specified order. Thus each record had to have a code (handle) by which it could be located in the computer file. After a record was found, the specific part of it that was to be updated had to be identifiable and accessible within the record itself. Computer records come in two basic formats: fixed length and variable length. Using the former of satisfy the updating requirement was the logical choice since most of the records would contain predictable elements of data; for example, author, title and publisher. A size limit was set that was large enough to accommodate the longest expected variable of each element. Each element then had its own field (fixed) in the same place in every record regardless of whether the field contained valid data for merely blanks supplied during translation. From a programming standpoint, in this application, fixed-length fields and records were considered much more convenient to work with than variable-length fields and records.

At this stage in the design of the machine record and the processing system the following points were decided upon:

1. Each record to have a unique number and was to contain fixed-length data fields.
2. A computer translation programme that would accept paper-tape input developed to:
   (i) translate the punched code into computer code,
   (ii) edit the translated data for validity, and (iii) format the data onto a magnetic tape for further processing.
3. A sort programme to arrange the records by their unique numbers.
4. Additional programmes to produce from the update master file output needed to satisfy the overall

requirements of the system; for example, a printed in-process list and a current accession list.

5. A processing programme to update the records.

It is pertinent to note that to explain more fully the computer translation programme (item 2), editing the data elements was possible with the parameters established for valid data in any given field. If a price field, for example was defined as one containing only digits or the letters GIFT, then a gift book coded as FREE in that field would be considered an error by the edit feature of the programme. Such invalid data were to be printed out in an error listing for correcting the input.

The formatting of the records was done by the programmer after the data elements had been established for the acquisitions system. It was here that the programmer played an important role. Balancing the needs of the system against the capabilities of the computer, he developed a tape format that would take maximum advantage of the machine's size, speed, and logic features to meet the requirements of the system. All but three of the fields in the supplied directly by the paper-tape input. Content in the three fields named CONNO (control number), CLAIMS, and STATUS, each indicated by arrows, is supplied entirely under computer programme control as a product of data processing but there is a difference between the data in CLAIMS and that in either CONNO or STATUS. The data in CLAIMS is *informative;* that is, if the record were printed out, the characters in the field would supply information directly to the reader without need of translation.

It should be remembered that one of the original demands made of the record was that it contain all the codes or *indicators* enabling it to be processed. CONNO and STATUS are examples of indicator fields. One feature of the system/360 computer that makes it a powerful data processing tool is its ability to access, test, and manipulate individual *bits* within a *byte*. A byte is composed of eight bits and represents one alphabetic or special character, two decimal digits or right binary bits of information. A byte for the letter A, for example, has the bits arranged thus: 1100000. By assigning each bit position a 1 or a 0 (on, off), eight separate conditions or any combination thereof may be carried in one byte.

The two fields STATUS and CONNO are each two-byte-long "message centers" with a combined potential for identifying 32 separate conditions. The data in STATUS and CONNO, then, are indicative rather than informative. If a particular record were printed out, its bit patterns, in STATUS and CONNO might or might not have a graphic representation on the printout and even if they did, the graphic would mean nothing in itself until it could be reduced to its own bit pattern and then interpreted. The combined four bytes of CONNO and STATUS may be used to indicate internally a record's condition and stage of processing throughout the time it is under programme control. Most conditions are best shown by the use of the CONNO and STATUS bit pattern "flags" rather than by relying on the presence or absence of information within the record. The presence of price data, for example, does not show that an item has been paid for, but a bit that can be set only when the invoice is cleared and paid shows the item as paid. Some of the conditions that the bits in CONNO and STATUS are sued to indicate are furnished below:

Bit Flags in CONNO and STATUS

	Bit	Condition
CONNO	0	On order
	1	Claimed
	2	Received—in process
	3	Invoice cleared and paid
	4	Cataloged
	5-15	Unassigned

STATUS	0	Departmental copy
	1	Reserve request
	2	General library copy
	3	Gift
	4	Gift plate
	5-15	Unassigned

The process of sorting is accomplished by utility programmes. These programmes usually are supplied by the computer manufacturer. They are very general and flexible with broad computer applications such as sorting a file, merging files, and punching, cards. There are usually few limitations on the use of such programmes and normally all the user needs to do is to describe the characteristics of his file and individual record to a particular utility programme. In using a utility programme for a sorting operation the input and output devices are designated first, the size of the file is given, then the individual record is specified as to its length, the position and length of the fields to be sorted (given in the order in which they are to be printed out—such as by order number, author, and title); and the sequence of the sort whether in ascending or descending order. Related to the utility programmes are the macro instructions. A definition of macro, "of or involving large quantities," implies its use. In computer terminology a macro is an instruction having the capability of generating more than one machine-language instruction and is incorporated under a coded name into the monitor system of the particular machine.

Thereafter when the macro's code name command is given, the monitor system expands it into the predefined set of instructions. Some commonly used macros are open, close, read, write, get, put, print, and punch. Generally in an actual instruction these macros would be followed by one or more file names showing what device or file the specified command is to act on. The macro facility in general provides convenient shortcuts for the programmer and wherever necessary he can write his own macros. If, for example, under certain conditions. *A* were to be replaced by *a* many times in several different programmes, the programmer could elect to write a macro called "replace" which would contain all the instructions necessary to replace *A* with *a*.

For example, a utility sort programme specifying publisher and title fields within the acquisitions transactions tape could arrange the file by publisher and for each publisher the titles on order to generate a list of in-process orders. The sort procedure operates with a nondestructive readout. At the conclusion of a sort there is not just a single file in a different order from that with which the sort began but two files. The original file is not erased or in any way destroyed n the process of being sorted. In the acquisitions system s utility sort is used prior to the update programme to produce a file sorted first by order number and then within the order number by the transaction codes to bring each record and its associated updating information together in a predetermined order for processing by the update programme.

As previously stated the system was to accept updating information in random order but a sort was necessary between the translation and update programmes because the records on both the master and transactions files are in sequential order to expedite matching of update data with the proper master record.

Update and Update Programme

Basically, the term "update" is very general and may be roughly equated to the expression "file maintenance." In a strict interpretation this involves modifying a master file with current information according to a specified procedure that could include an exchange of characters for blanks or if the master record is being corrected, an exchange of valid characters for invalid ones. Using presorted input the steps of the file maintenance programme are to match each transaction to the proper master record, identify the type of transaction (price or date received) an enter new data or corrected data. The designation "update programme" was given the file maintenance procedure of updating combined with other procedures.

While the primary achievement of the update programme is a current on-order file, such features as bit testing and manipulation and speed of processing make it practical to satisfy other system requirements concurrently. Output is produced as a by-product of processing each record including such useful procedures as statists on books ordered and received, reports on the amounts encumbered and spent from various funds, list of errors in input data, and a file of items for which processing has been completed.

Changes in the Acquisitions System

From the design of the acquisitions system under discussion a core of programmed processing emerged that included facets of the operations in the acquisitions sub-systems. In a computer-based system the core of programme processing will often cut across the boundaries of subsystem as they existed before the new system was initiated. In this acquisitions system the various operations and functions of the manually maintained subsystems had to be realigned with the revised subsystems for the newly designed system to be effective. As a case in point we can consider the four acquisitions subsystem of preorder searching, ordering, accounting and reporting, and receiving and checking. The changes within the redesigned system are shown as follows:

Before	*After*
Preorder searching	Unchanged
Ordering	Ordering, I/O preparation and processing
Accounting and reporting	Data processing
Receiving and checking	Receiving, I/O preparation and processing

Notably, at east one major operation of ordering, the maintenance of an in-process file, has been taken over by the new subsystem data processing. Similarly the operation of maintaining account balances, previously maintained by accounting and reporting is now absorbed by data processing. The original requirements of the system are still being satisfied and further the new system has the potential of satisfying increases in these requirements.

In planning the design of the acquisition system that we have been discussing, the total-systems approach was used in considering the placing of the routine and data processing operations of the system under machine control.

As part of the design of the computer-based acquisitions system it was decided that punched cards for the circulation system should be produced from the magnetic-tape acquisitions record file after it has been updated with call numbers. The programme produced a master machine-readable circulation card for a currently processed book. This card, which lists the accession number, the author or title, and the call number, was inserted into the book.

This procedure was the first phase in implementing the computer-based circulation system while still operating under manual conditions. Because, new books are expected to circulate more than the old and because most new and circulating materials are equipped with punched cards, the automated circulation system should be fully operational at the time of installation. Another output produced after the machine-readable acquisitions record has been updated with call numbers is the accessions list. It is arranged by call number and provides the author and title of each book. This bimonthly listing is distributed by the reference librarians as a current awareness service to users.

It is different from the in-process list in that the accessions list is shelf list of newly cataloged books. It is intended to a allow persons interested in a given subject to scan a pertinent block of call numbers and be aware of new library acquisitions that may related to his field of interest. As a requirement of the machine-readable acquisitions file it was decided that the file should be a historical (retrospective) record primarily for the possible use of these records as the means to find and "lift" full machine-readable cataloging data from MARC tapes or from some other library's cataloging data bank. This is seen as a way to save time and effort when the decision is made to convert existing cataloging records to machine-readable form.

COMPUTER-BASED SERIALS SYSTEM

Basically, designing a computer-based serials system follows the prescribed pattern: the establishment of requirements, the provision of forms and the determination of the manual and machine procedures that will satisfy the requirements.

In fact, the *primary* requirement of the serials system is to provide users with an accurate and current file of the library's serials holdings including all the necessary bibliographic information. In the instance we shall discuss, the file will be a union catalogue containing the data required on all serials in both the general library and the branch libraries.

The data in this file should be available not only in the general library but also in branches and to other possible users. *Second,* the system should be able to provide the means whereby the user as well as the library staff may request and receive within a reasonable time special catalogs or reports of the serials holdings by such categories as call number, language, and subject; and it should also provide special listings by publishers, vendors, types of serials, status (such as active, inactive), and by all condition of receipt (gift, purchase, or exchange).

Third, the system should be able to guarantee that all issues not received by the library will be claimed promptly and on a set schedule and also that the renewal of all serial subscriptions will be controlled by the system. *Fourth*, the system should be able to predict the time of receipt of a journal issue with accuracy thereby establishing a positive control over the timely receipt of all issues. *Fifth,* the system must be able to maintain and control all the accounting records necessary for its own internal use and be able to report to the comptroller the information required for payment of invoices. *Sixth,* the system should be able to provide the binding department with necessary information and records for those journals that are to be bound. It also should be able to provide such information and records on a scheduled basis in order to maintain an even workload for the binding staff. *Seventh,* the serials system should have the ability to handle the many changes that occur in the various serials titles.

Compiling Serials Records

With the establishment of the requirements of the system the next task is to determine what information is necessary as input to the computer system if it is to satisfy the requirements as outlined. It should be determined where this information can be obtained if existing records are inadequate and what format and under what restrictions the input of information should be placed. The input worksheet should be designed to obtain the maximum amount of information with the least cost. The form finally adopted should contain all the information necessary for the functioning of the system.

The original step in compiling the serials record starts when the compiler removes from the existing central serials file the holdings record, or the current check-in record, or both. The holdings card indicates any title changes or title variations. If changes have occurred, the compiler removes from the central serials file those cross-referenced records pertaining to the title variations or changes in question; that is, all of the library's records covering the history of this particular title are removed. Referring to the serials control record worksheet, the first box in the upper left-hand corner carries the Dewey call number obtained from the library's record. In the case of the call number, where there have been title changes or there are multiple subscriptions and the same call number has been used for each new change or subscription, it is necessary for the compiler to add to the call number a hyphen and an additional digit (–1, –2, –3, and so forth) to identify each title within the computer record. The next step in compilation is to verify the official title, if possible, in the *National Union Catalogue* (NUC).

If it is found there, it is used as the main entry for input to the computer. The LC call number, if found in NUC, is recorded in the upper right-hand corner of the form. The compiler also indicates under the word "verified" the volume and year of NUC in which the title was verified. If the publication is not found in NUC, the next step is to search in the *Union List of Serials*. Here again, if the title is found, the entry is accepted as the main entry. If the entry is not found in the *Union List of Serials*, the search is continued in *New Serials Titles* and if necessary, in *Ulrich's International Periodicals Directory*.

The next item on the form is the short title which cannot exceed forty characters in length. The short title should conform to the title as it appears on the cover of the serial itself as an aid to checking in the issue. The abbreviations for periodical literature provided by the United States of American Standards Institute are used in establishing the short title.

Proceeding down the form the next blocks are Holdings-start and Holdings-end. This information is obtained from the library's holdings record. The information for the Publication-start and Publicationend blocks is obtained from NUC or the *Union List of Serials* and if not located, it is taken from other bibliographic sources. The items in the next two horizontal lines of data are coded. The following defines the data elements and supplies examples of some of the code structure.

Keyword	*Description of Data Element*
LIB (Library)	Refers to the particular library or collection that maintains the file of a journal (00 = general library, 41 = business and economics).
LOC (Location)	The location in the library. This is used primarily to indicate where the journal is to be shelved (2 = current display rack). It is also used to identify the location to which it is routed previous to shelving (A = table of contents photocopy service).
LANG (Language)	The language or languages in which the journal is published (01 = Chinese, 20 = multilingual with English).
TYPE	Refers to form of publication—that is, abstracts, periodicals, transactions (10 = index or abstract, 40 = proceedings).
STAT (Status)	Refers to variations such as active, ceased publication, discontinued subscription, title change (1 = ceased publication).
RET (Retention)	Refers to the period of time of retention and conditions under which a journal is kept, that is, one year and discard, two years in branch and forward to general library, and similar variations in handling (3 = discard after three years).
BIND (Bindery)	Refers to the commercial binder used.
COLOR (Colour)	The four-digit code for the color of binding cloth to be used.
ISSUE PHY VOL (Issues per physical volume)	Defines the number of issues that are bound in a physical volume.
INDEX	Refers to when and how the index is received and where it is found in the journal (0 = no index, 4 = separate, free on request).
INDEXED IN	Obtained from *Ulrich's International Periodicals Directory*. Here is indicated indexing services in which the journal

	is indexed or abstracted (175 = *Reader's Guide*, 095 = *Fuel Abstracts*).
FREQ (Frequency)	Defines the frequency of publication of each title- that is, monthly, weekly, quarterly, and so forth (01 = weekly, 16 = bimonthly).
NO. OF ISSUE VOL	The number of issues per bibliographic volume.
CC (Claim Control)	Indicates the waiting period at end of which an issue is claimed (21 = one month late).
JFMA.... (Jan, Feb, Mar, Apr)	Used for forecasting the time of receipt of issues so that the computer can produce the check-in punched card in advance of receipt.
REC (Receipt)	The condition of receipt— for example, gift, group purchase, membership, group purchase, exchange (4 = gift, 9 = group purchase.
GROUP NO.	If, for example, a journal is received as part of the package plan with the American Chemical Society, a unique two-digit number is assigned to American Chemical Society and each title received in the package plan is assigned that number so that all journals received under the plan can be identified as a group for accounting purposes.
DATE START	Refers to the date that the last subscription started and controls the renewal of the subscription.
LAST PAYMENT	Used to verify that a title was renewed previously and when.
SUB LGT (Subscription length)	Used in conjunction with DATE START to determine next renewal date of a title.
REQ DEPT (Requesting department)	Used in connection with the FUND NO for accounting and statistical purposes. The LIB codes are used in identifying departments that have requested subscriptions either for housing in the departments or in the general library.
FUND NO. (Fund number)	Refers to the account against which the subscription is charged.

SUBS PRICE (Subscription price)	Refers to the cost of a subscription or last renewal.
ISSUING AGENCY	Full name and address of the issuing agency (publisher).
SUPPLIER	The name and address of the supplier or vendor when different from the issuing agency.

Further, the balance of the serials control record worksheet is used for the additional bibliographic control data desired in this system. Entered in the last part of the form are the S-SUBJECT entries as found in NUC for each title. If the title is not found in NUC, the librarians revising the records must assign at least one compatible subject to each title. The A-ADDED entries used are those given in NUC excluding the added entry for editor. Indication of title changes follow the subject and added entries. If there is a title change with the new title continuing old volume numbering, such title change is designated F-FORMERLY ISSUED AS, or C-CONTINUED AS. On the other hand a title change with its own and new volume numbering is designated Z-SUPERSEDES or X-SUPER-SEDED BY. If two titles are merged to form a new title, both titles would be entered under the code M-MERGED.

Any necessary notes that will facilitate the user's approach to a serial title are entered under the code N-NOTES. After the information has been compiled on the serials control record worksheets, it must be verified and, if necessary, revised.

After the data on the worksheet have been revised and all corrections made, it is forwarded to the data processing operator who prepares the input tape using the paper-tape typewriter. Reading from the serials control record worksheet the data processing operator types this information on a serials control record form simultaneously producing paper tape containing all of the compiled information. There are three ways of correcting information entered into the paper tape : (i) If a character is incorrectly typed, the operator immediately may insert a delete character to erase the error and continue with the typing. (ii) The operator at any time during the typing of a record may insert a special code which will indicate to the computer that this record is to be disregarded and that a substitute record will be entered. (iii) At the end of the record the operator has the opportunity to correct any field that may have been typed in error by inserting the field control number followed by the correct information; a computer programme will then insert the corrected information furnished by the operator, in the field indicated. Each serials control record form produced concurrently with the paper tape is proofread for typographical errors at the end of the day's production. Any errors that are found during proofreading may be corrected by the operator at any time.

The correction procedure is to punch five items into the paper tape; first, the code indicating to the programme that this is a correction record; second, a code indicating the type of correction (A for an addition to a record, C for a correction to some field within the record, or D to delete some item of information from the record); third, the Dewey call number of the title to be corrected; fourth, the field control number of the field in error; and fifth, the corrected information.

The correction record on paper tape will be used to make the necessary corrections, additions, or deletions to the machine-readable record identified by the Dewey call number.

Serial Record Load System

The next phase of the serials automation system consists of designing the programme required initially to load and format the serials records. Serial Record Load System, illustrates the generalized system. Requirements of the system are : (i) to produce a report for verification of each serials record loaded to date and arranged in Dewey call-number sequence; (ii) to produce a report for verification of each serials record loaded in the current run; and (iii) to produce a report of any record or records containing erroneous information (errors, duplicated records).

Inputs to the system are : (i) a paper tape containing new serials records; and (ii) A paper tape containing corrections, additions, and deletions to be made in existing computer records.

The first requirement of the programme is to produce a report listing each error found in the editing procedure. Based on the editing report the data processing operator will correct the errors (as described previously) and will re-enter the corrections into the computer in a later run of the translate and edit programme. The second requirement is to assemble the input data into proper format as developed for the master serials record. Master Serials Record, shows the layout of the computer record which consists of five sections. The first section of the record is fixed in length and contains the majority of the data characterizes as "basic identification and control data."

The second section is fixed in length and contains the accounting data including a five-year historical record of the payment of each serial subscription. (A five-year average of the increase in serials cost should permit forecasting of serials budgets with a high degree of reliability.) The third section of the master serials record, variable in length, contains bibliographical information on each title.

This includes the official entry, all subject entries, selected added entries, title changes, and all notes. Each of these items is variable in length and each field, except the official entry field, may contain more than one entry. For example, there might be two or three subject entries for a particular title.

The fourth section, variable in length, is the claiming and receipt section. This portion of the record is generated internally by the check-in programme at the time it forecasts the receipt of each issue of a title. The fifth section, variable in length, contains the binding information, the greater portion of which is created by the check-in programme at the time the updated information is received by the computer.

Thus, the inputs to the programme are (i) paper tape of new serials records; and (ii) paper tape of correction records. Output of the programme are : (i) serials transactions file on magnetic tape containing the new titles that have been loaded during a given run plus corrections to previous titles that were loaded at an earlier date and (ii) the editing report indicating what errors the computer has found during the edit process. Functions of the programme are : (i) to read in the data from the paper-tape reader (since the codes that are produced by the paper-tape typewriter are not the same as the code structure used in the computer, the characters on this tape must be translated into the appropriate machine language); and (ii) to edit each field of the serials record to make sure that it conforms to the requirements of length and content of the field and that the information as presented is valid. For example, under the area LIB (library) it is possible that the operator type a code that is not a valid departmental code— or in typing the MAIN ENTRY an invalid character was used or for an active serial the FREQ (frequency) code was omitted. Thus each item on the form, where it is possible, will be edited for validity and completeness.

The requirement of the programme is to sort the new serial record file into Dewey call-number sequence. Input to the programme is the serials transactions file produced in the translate and edit programme and containing new and corrected serials records. Output of the programme is a sorted serials transactions file containing new and corrected serials records in Dewey call-number sequence. Function of the programme is to sort the records contained in the magnetic-tape files into a desired order or sequence.

Requirements of the programme are : (i) to generate a new master serials record file; (ii) to make corrections to existing records; and (iii) to eliminate duplicate records. Inputs to the programme are : (i) sorted serials transactions file of new and corrected serials record; and (ii) a sorted master file of existing serials records.

Outputs of the programme are:

(i) a magnetic tape file containing all records, existing and new,

(ii) a printed listing of new and corrected titles loaded in this run, and

(iii) a printed listing of erroneous records.

Functions of the programme are: (i) to merge old and new records on the two input tapes into one output master file; and (ii) to correct any record in the old tape file prior to generating the new tape file.

Catalogue Report Generator System

The catalogue report generator system allows flexibility to the library staff and to the user by obtaining information from the system in the sequence and in the format wanted. This system is a medium by which users can exploit the informational potentialities of the serials control system. Generalized Systems Chart of the Catalogue Report Generator System, outlines the programmes and their interrelationships required in the preparation of specified printed catalogs and reports.

Requirements of the system are : (i) to provide the user with an accurate and current catalogue of the serials holdings containing the necessary bibliographic information; Serials Catalogue) and (ii) to provide the means whereby the user as well as staff members may request and receive special catalogs or reports of the serials holdings within a reasonable time.

Serials Listing by Subject; Serials Listing by Call No; Serials Listing Departmental Libraries- Arch). Inputs to the system are: (i) the master magnetic tape file of serial records and (ii) the data control punched cards for selection of data and desired sequence and format of the report. Outputs of the system are printed catalogs or reports. When printout of these catalogs or reports is required, it is only necessary for the serials librarian to indicate this by the appropriate code in a control card. The generator system based on this code will automatically select from the master record the data required for the printing of a given list.

The requirement of the programme is selection of desired information from the master file by means of the data control cards. Inputs of the programme are : (i) a the master file of serials records and (b) data control card for each item of information that is to appear in a given report. The output of the programme is a magnetic-tape file containing information for each of the requested reports, or catalogs, or both. Functions of the programme are : (i) stripping from the master serials record file the data required for the printing of catalogs or special reports as specified by the data control cards; and (ii) formatting such information and transferring the resulting record to an output work tape.

The requirement of this programme is to sort each of the report work tapes into desired sequence specified by the sort control card. Inputs to the programme are : (i) the report work tapes created by the catalogue report generator programme; and (ii) the sort control cards that define the order in which records are to appear. The output of the programme is a file of the records to be printed as a report or catalogue.

The requirement of the programme is to print in desired format any standard catalogs or special reports. Inputs to the programme are : (i) the sorted report file; and (ii) the print control card that defines the format in which the information is to appear.

Operating Systems

So far we have described in some detail the systems for compiling the original input to the serials system for setting up the master record file and for correcting this file and for setting up the reporting system required to produce the necessary reports or catalogs. The primary purpose of the serials operating systems is to provide efficient and accurate control of all records and the transactions.

Systems charts of the monthly and weekly operating systems, outline the programmes and their interrelationships that are necessary to fulfill the following requirements:

1. Predict the time of receipt of the journal thereby establishing a positive control over the timely receipt of all issues.
2. Guarantee that all issues not received by the library will be claimed promptly and on a set schedule and that the renewal of all serials will be controlled by the system.
3. Maintain and control the accounting records necessary for the serials system internally as well as report to the comptroller the information required for payment of invoices.
4. Handle the many changes that occur in the various serials titles.
5. Provide the binding department with the necessary information and records for those titles that are to be bound.

In fact, Outputs of the operating systems are : (i) an updated master file of all serials records; (ii) punched control cards anticipating receipt of issues; (iii) reports for controlling, claiming, renewals, and binding; and (iv) statistical and accounting reports. The operated systems work within three time frames: monthly, weekly, and daily. We shall now review functions that are performed by both the computer and the clerical.

Operating Functions

This section describes the function of the staff of the serials system and the data processing operator in maintaining records.

1. *Check-in:* When an issue is received, the serials clerk removes from the punched-card file the corresponding check-in card for the particular volume and issue. In the case of an irregular publication it is necessary to record on the check-in card (if not there already) the volume and issue number, adding the month and year of publication. The clerk marks the call number on the issue and checks for changes such as title and frequency in the journal. If variations are not found, the check-in card and is forwarded to the data processing operator.

If changes have occurred, they are recorded on the serials control record worksheet, indicating the call number and the changes in the appropriate fields. The check-in card and the worksheet are forwarded to the data processing operator who, using the auxiliary punched-card reader attached to the paper-tape typewriter, enters the check-in card data into the paper tape.

The call number, issue, month, and year are punched into the paper tape as input to the weekly run of the check-in programme. If corrections or changes to a given title are made, the data processing operator holds these until the end of the day or week when the correction tape for input to the translate and edit programme is produced.

2. *Ordering of New Serial Titles* : On receipt of the first issue of a new title the serials librarian prepares a serials control

record worksheet that is forwarded to the data processing operator for entry of the new title into the system.

3. *Renewal of Subscriptions* : The renewal control cards and the renewal reports are received from the computer. The renewal punched card is filed. The renewal report is verified and two copies forwarded to the supplier or the publisher for the renewal of the indicated titles. When the invoice, the invoice is received, the renewal control card for each title on the invoice, the invoice number, and the amount of the renewal are posted to the renewal control card.

The renewal control report is checked for each title and the renewal control card is then forwarded to the data processing operator. The operator duplicates the prepunched information on the renewal control card and key punches the new information (invoice date and number and renewal cost) and simultaneously produces a punched paper tape with this information. This is accomplished by using a key punch that is cabled to the paper-tape typewriter.

4. *Binding Control* : On receipt of the binding control list and the control cards the binding department uses the control list as its worksheet for the coming month. The jour-nals are taken from the shelves and checked for completeness. Binding orders are then prepared for the completed volumes. It is the responsibility of the binding clerk to submit correction reports for any issues or indexes found missing.

5. *Claiming of Serial Issues*: The weekly run of the check-in programme prints out the claim notices. These notices are reviewed prior to mailing because notice may have been received from the supplier or publisher that item will be delayed. In such event the computer record is updated. If the claim is routine, the notice is forwarded to the supplier. On receipt of the claimed

issue the check-in card for that issue is removed from the file and forwarded to the data processing operator.

The monthly run of the check-in programme is the key to the successful fulfillment of the operating system. It is the function of this programme to forecast the transactions that are to occur within the serials system for the coming month and to produce the reports and control cards that are needed to handle successfully these transactions. The monthly run of the check-in programme has specific functions that must be performed.

1. A forecasting must be made of the issues to be received for each of the active during the coming month. Utilizing the FREQ (frequency) data in conjunction with the months of publication data (JFM....field) the programme will determine whether an issue is to be received or claimed; the check-in programme will determine, when possible, the volume and issue numbers to received in the coming period. A control card will be punched for each issue to be received. Simultaneously the programme will post in the waiting receipt and claims section of the master record the control data for each particular issue. The check-in cards will be filed in the serials department awaiting receipt of the issue.

2. A listing must be produced of all titles whose subscriptions are to be renewed during the second month following the monthly run. (For example, during the June run the computer will forecast those titles to be renewed during August of that year.) This programme determines the renewal date by utilizing the date of last renewal found in the DATE SUBS START (date subscription start field and the period of the last subscription from the SUBS LGT (subscription length) field, both found in the accounting data section of the master record. The renewal report is produced by vendor or by publisher showing the titles that should be renewed in the period. The report contains the call number, the

title, the last renewal date, the subscription length, and the estimated price of renewal. At this point, programme also produces a control card for each item being renewed. The control card contains the call number and short title. The programme also posts to the accounting data control section the renewal cost incurred.

3. A binding report is necessary for those titles with sufficient consecutive issues to warrant binding into a physical volume. A control card is produced for each volume to be bound and an indication is made in the binding control section of the master record that an order has been issued for binding.

4. Accounting reports are required for the financial control of the system. These reports are based on encumbrances incurred by each fund and department account. In order to obtain a net balance for each fund and department account at the end of each month the encumbrances are adjusted to actual cost on receipt of invoices.

5. The programme must generate monthly statistics of the number of new titles added and their cost, the number of renewals and the estimated cost of renewals, the number of issues received, the number of bound volumes added to the serials collection, and other statistical information.

For all titles frequency of receipt is irregular the check-in programme will, on the receipt of an issue, produce a check-in card for the next arrival. This card contains only the call number and the short title of the issue and, if possible, the volume and the issue number but not the month or year.

Remember, at end of each week all input paper tapes for the serials system are forwarded to the computer center for entry into the weekly run of the check-in programme. These tapes are processed through the translate and edit programme.

The output of this translate and edit programme. The output of this sort programme, arranged by call number and type of transaction, is the input to the weekly run of the check-in programme.

The function of the check-in programme is to post all transactions that have occurred to the serials master record file. The primary output of the weekly check-in programme is the claim notices. During the weekly run the programme audits each record, comparing the date of a forecasted arrival in the WAITING RECEIPT sector of the record to the CLAIM CTL (claim control) date. If the issue is overdue, a claim is issued. If a subsequent published issue is received prior to the receipt of an earlier published issue, a claim is issued is received, the WAITING RECEIPT sector of the record is cleared and the issue is posted to the binding control section of the record. The output of the weekly run is the updated serials master control file that is always the source of all printed reports.

A critical operation within the serials system is the check-in and claiming of journal issues. There is an alternative to the punched card, paper-tape check-in and claiming operations in the computer-based serials system. The direct use of the punched from the check-in file as input to the weekly run of the check-in programme could be a more efficient way to update the master serials record file. If the punched cards produced by the computer for the check-in operation contained the required information for check-in, the intermediate step of paper tape might well be eliminated. If this were done, no translate programme would be necessary because punched cards do not require this. This phase of the weekly programme would only require a card-to-tape utility programme. Another alternative could be that instead of punched cards, a monthly printout listing of expected journal issues could be used. After a journal issue is received, it could be crossed off the printed list, marked, and sent to the shelves. At the end of the month the printout would be sent to the claiming subsystem for processing. Those titles not crossed off would require a claims notice. The initial notice, both to the vendor and the computer record, would be produced on the paper-tape typewriter.

Subsequent claim notices would be issued by the claims programme under computer control. Updating the computer record with information about the issues that have been received would be accomplished by the computer not being notified. If no notice were received, programming would provide for the computer record to be updated automatically on the assumption that the issue had been received.

COMPUTER BASED CIRCULATION SYSTEM

As suggested by the theme total systems concepts are viewed and evaluated to indicate their importance in designing a computer-based circulation system. Planning with total systems concepts in mind should disclose most of the ramifications that will occur after implementation of a new system.

The phrase "total system," as used here, concerns itself with more than the immediate library system or the overall parent administrative system. Rather it is meant to designate the symbiotic relationships within the library and the general relationships of the library with society; that is, it is meant to deal with the interrelationships or interdependence among systems that affect one another and in many instances justify and facilitate the existence and performance of systems. Interdependence is the key word describing the inner workings of systems within a total system.

A limited, two-dimensional representation showing one phase of interdependence of systems is illustrated in total system. This diagram illustrates some of the interrelationships that do exist.

General society, all inclusive, is the source not only for the people who are to manage the library but also for the library users and the supply of outside supporting services and materials to the library. When viewed in closer perspective the interdependent systems of the library in become obvious. Stylized, relationships between the systems within the total library are shown encompassed by the administration and planning system. Circulation is depicted as logically interrelated with the reference system and the cataloging system. From the latter newly processed library materials are received and controlled by the circulation system in order to provide the library's users with ready access. The location symbols assigned and indexes prepared and maintained by cataloging are used by the circulation system and by the library users to locate and relocate desired items.

One of the relationships between acquisitions and cataloging in which the one furnishes the material for the other to process so as to make it readily accessible to the library user and to other systems, further serves as an illustration of the total systems concept. Reciprocally the records that cataloging maintains allow acquisitions to search each purchase request effectively before ordering to avoid unwanted duplication of material work.

Design

When the circulation system is accepted as a system that is directly interdependent with other systems within the library as well as with outside systems (that is, the user), a more lucid understanding of the place of the circulation system within the total library system may be realized. It should also become increasingly clear that the design of a new system with its stated demands and requirements and its inputs/outputs will have direct bearing in varying degree on all the other systems within the total system. Therefore it becomes very important in designing a new system to be fully aware of what immediate and long-term effects a new printed form, method or procedure will have on existing cosystems.

In considering the design of a computer-based loan system it should at least be able to emulate the worthwhile elements of the existing systems. These elements, probably common to all circulation systems, include the ability to :

1. Indicate what book is out and who has it.
2. Indicate the date the book was taken out and the date it is to be returned.
3. Allow for a daily count of circulation activity by type of material and possibly by the status of the user.
4. Search for missing books, and if found or not, notify the requestor of the book's availability.
5. Charge out and discharge library material.
6. Allow for reserving charged-out library material.
7. Maintain records of overdue books and issue notices as required.
8. Allow for a daily updating of the master file of outstanding circulation by interfiling the daily transactions.
9. Provide on users' notices the call number, title, and due date of the requested material.
10. Facilitate recall of charged-out material prior to its due date.
11. Enable the library to know the user's identify prior to borrowing any material.

Accepting the necessity for maintaining the objectives of the existing circulation system, the computer-based system could be designed by the analyst to gain a variety of improvements in the maintenance and accessibility of circulation records and more meaningful statistical records. In addition to improving on present objectives the computer-based circulation system should be designed to be flexible enough to:

1. Ascertain the user's identity and be able to correlate by statistical analysis, his subject background with the type of material he charges out.
2. Answer a user's enquiry as to the status of a book (out, in, missing) by current printouts arranged variously by author or title, call number, and borrower, including in each listing the date the material was charged out and is to be returned.
3. Provide work-unit statistics to indicate hourly and daily workloads.
4. Maintain a historical file of loan transaction records for use in periodic statistical studies.
5. Be as mechanical as possible in its charge and discharge operations so as not to be dependent to any appreciate extent on manual keying or writing functions and thus make charge and discharge operations as rapid and free of error as possible.
6. Allow for *portable* terminal data collection devices for use in inventorying the book collection and perhaps to allow for user self-charging of material.
7. Take into account short circulation periods, anywhere from a few minutes to several hours, allowing for class reserve books to be controlled by the computer-based circulation system. (This may be best performed in an on-line system).
8. Provide for continuing analysis of the book collection by frequency of use by subject and subject background of user so as to evaluate collection growth and adequacy.
9. Indicate the retrospective and current number of uses of any book within the library's collection to facilitate the

ordering of additional copies of materials or the weeding out of inactive material.

10. Permit expeditious inventorying of the collection with machine readable records.
11. Maintain statistical records of user requests for missing books.
12. Allow for conversion to an online circulation system.
13. Be able to generate on request lists of books charged to individual users.
14. Machine produce on request and as needed recall and overdue notices.
15. Analyze the use made of class reserve reading material.

Remarkably, not only should the systems analyst be aware of what objectives the circulation system should fulfill, he should also be able to evaluate the commercially available mechanical data collection (input) devices best suited to realize the total systems concepts in the computer-based circulation system. Along with the decision made regarding the type of input devices to be used to capture the transaction record, a master punched book card (the input) for each circulating item, probably an 80-column punched card, should be produced with enough information to identify the book. If the bibliographic data is already computer based, it is only a matter of stripping the necessary information from the existing computer record and producing the punched bok card, interpreting the Hollerith code to make the card man-readable, and inserting it into the book.

An example of planning for the future is provided in the case of the library system that has used no book cards, even under the manual system, but still provided a book card pocket in the back of each book in the planned event that punched cards would be used as master book cards in a computer-based circulation system. If the cataloging system is at present converting its records to machine-readable form, the master book card could be an economical by-product of the conversation process. As the shelf list is converted selected information would be punched into the punched card to create a master book card could for the circulation system.

If no machine-readable bibliographic records exist, the conversion of records to machine-readable form to produce the master book cards is a costly and critical operation prior to the implementation of the computer-based circulation system.

Master Book Card

Here it must be remembered that provided that a machine-readable record can be produced, the analyst should define the data to be carried on each master book card. He has less than 80 columns with which to uniquely identify the book because some of the card space is allocated for the identification number of the user, which will appear on the transaction card combined with the data from the master book card.

Therefore the information contained in the master book card and that added to the transaction card, although minimal, should allow for:

1. Positive identification of the specific book by the master book card. The order or accession number or the full call number, or both, including volume, part, copy, and so forth, would appear to be necessary.
2. *The due date* the computer programme can take this into account and provide the due date on the printout.
3. Enough bibliographic information to enable the user and the library staff to identify the book by author or title, or both, in a printout list of loan transactions. It may not be necessary for this information to be punched into the master book card because a machine-readable

shelf list in computer storage can be used either in real-time (immediate access) or in an off-line situation for complete identification of the book if the call number or the order number is used as the key to the entire bibliographic record.

An advantage to creating a master book card that is bibliographically self-sufficient is that it allows for generation of computer printouts directly as requested. The printing out of the outstanding circulation file can be accomplished by sorting and revising only the information pertinent to circulation without referencing the entire store of cataloging data.

The data to be carried by the machine-readable user identification card should be specified by the analyst. If properly designed, this card serves as an excellent example of application of the total systems design concept. For the purposes of the library the identification card would be Hollerith coded with some identifying number that would serve as the key to each user's name and address and other pertinent information in a separate machine-readable file. This key number, which would be punched into the user's card, should have certain characteristics:

1. It should be short enough for the identification card and for the remaining space on the master book card when combined in a transaction card.
2. It also should take into account the accessibility of already existing machine-readable borrower files or other machine-readable files carrying this type of information that could be used to provide addresses and other data for collection development studies. If no machine-readable files exist, it is a matter of converting manual borrower or user files.

Further, identification card to be carried by each user should be provided or an existing card modified to meet the demands of the new system. This card requires key punching and if this is not amenable to an already existing card, a new one will be needed. If a new identification card is required, it should be designed to carry : (i) positive identification of the user by a photograph, name, the Hollerith coded identification number, and possibly the person's signature and (ii) any additional information that is compatible with other uses of the card outside of the library. In support of the total systems concept the identification card should be designed to be useful, if possible, in other systems. By embossing the name and birthdate of the carrier on the card it can be used as a "charge plate"; and by providing a photograph and signature it can serve as a very compact general-use identification card.

In a university situation such a card would find application in library, bookstore, registration, and student activities transactions. The most important characteristic of identification number to be punched into the card is the adaptability it will or should have in existing machine-readable identification files in various systems. Therefore special consideration should be given to the machine-readable number to be used: is it to be a locally unique number or a nationally unique one like the Social Security number? In support of the nationally unique number the implications of the increasing interest and activity in shared library resources indicate the need for universal identification.

For example, in a network of libraries if a number of the cooperating libraries implement computer-based circulation systems and users from any one of these borrow books from various libraries in the system, the identification number should be machine-compatible throughout the system. This obviously necessitates a machine-readable central address file accessible to the cooperating libraries.

The format and content of the master book card and user identification are important to the contributions of the circulation system to the total library systems goals. This is in terms of the circulation system's ability to contribute effectively to the administration of the library and to collection development for best service to users. If a library is to capitalize on the statistical information available from daily circulation transaction records, some planned means of making use of this data should be provided. The materials circulated are obviously an indication of user subject and intellectual interests and development.

A variety of statistical records can be supplied by a functionally designed computer-based circulation system. Continuing statistical analysis can serve to signal and predict fluctuations in demands being placed on the library. Therefore data collection as a by-product of the circulation control system should be designed to be sensitive to the subtle changes in user requirements and expectations. The result of such an approach will verify the aptness of the techniques already in use to attain the library's service goals or it may show the conventional techniques to be inadequate. In order to analyze properly information gathered the data collection function needs to be designed to: (i) incorporate flexibility and compatibility in the gathered data to generate needed reports; (ii) balance economic limitations against statistical reports clearly required in terms of the broadness of their application; and (iii) consider the needs and demands of the user, the types of users, and the ecology of the library. A library network's requirements may well differ from those of any one member library.

Device

The mechanical input device in a computer-based loan system should be able to generate the necessary data for computer input. Apart from expeditiously accepting and processing the inserted master book card and the user's card, the machine should be able to withstand extensive use in repeated charging and discharging functions. It would seem that the more simple the machine's construction and the more independent it is of auxiliary equipment, the less chance there is of it failing. It should have the feature of being able to go on line.

Regarding the routine operations in which the machine will be involved, the discharging of books may be a problem area under certain conditions. In a one-card system the master card is used to produce the charge and discharge record for the input to the computer and in doing so requires that the book always stay with the master card. As a solution to this problem a two-card system produced by the input device is suggested.

Two cards are produced from the master book card : (i) a charge-out card that contains the same data as the transaction card and is placed in the book pocket along with the master card; and (ii) a transaction record card that serves as computer input. By this method the charge card can be removed from the returned book and the book sent immediately to the selves. The charge-out card serves to clear the computer record by matching with the transaction record as it appears in the computer.

By defining the necessary data to be incorporated in each master book card and user card the analyst should be able to extract a number of valuable statistical use studies and measures from the loan record. For example, because there are no precise means of ascertaining stack or in house use of books, those charged out should have significance in measuring the use of the collection and in collection development. Because the computer can readily provide records of actual use and non-use of books, this has direct bearing on collection development by the reference system. If a subject represented by a group of books is no longer referred to, the purchase of new materials in that subject field may be questioned.

Effective collection development through awareness of use should also provide data for subject profiles of specialized users, augmented and confirmed by personal interviews. If circulation records reveal that a title is used extensively, additional copies may be automatically purchased. Within the cumulative circulation statistical record, book use can be measured and classified by call number and perhaps, preferably, by means of the subject "tracings" in the computerized shelf list correlated with the subject background of users. From observation of circulation trends suggested reading lists of currently appearing titles could be produced as an awareness service in the subject areas of readers' interests.

Through the use of statistics it would be possible to predict inductively by any subject's use or non-use the significant growth or decline of interest by library users. This could be a direct aid in the library's book-selection subsystem. In most, if not all libraries, the administration is in competition for increased budgets with other units and offices of the governing administration. The library administration should be able to demonstrate through quantitative and qualitative use records of the library's collection the need for an increased book budget. These use studies may also indicate need for a decrease in or shifting of acquisitions funds that may have been wanted in maintaining unused subject collections.

An additional operation that would be dependent on a computer-based circulation record and shelf list would be that of inventorying the collection entirely or on a sampling basis. Records of user queries foe missing books in a given area might indicate the need for an inventory of that area.

The weeding of library collections is often neglected. By comparing a computer listing of materials used in the last five years, for example, against a machine-readable shelf, a list of material not loaned in that period could be produced. This list could serve as the basis of a weeding operation. This appears to be a better method than basing reasons to discard materials or place them in inactive storage on general age-use mathematical models.

If as one of the primary steps in implementing a computer-based system all master book cards are prepared but not inserted into the books until they are charged out, the remaining file of master book cards not inserted after x number of years would indicate those books not circulated in the predesignated period of time. This remaining file could be processed to produce a list of books eligible for weeding operations either withdrawal or referral to inactive storage. As implied previously circulation transaction records are one of the best sources of information about collection-use patterns. Other means of ascertaining use, including on-site observation and the counting of unshelved books on tables, may be too limited and may not cover the overall aspects that an extensive collection of computerized circulation records could provide. The percentage of books ten years old or older found on study tables in a two-week period and used as the basis to extrapolate a general statement on the entire collection's use does not necessarily provide sufficient guidance for weeding of a collection.

Under the total-system concept and the management by exception principle all facets of collection use are considered or may be considered. This reveals not only the extent of use of older books but also an itemized listing of these books, their subjects background of their users. By exploiting the full capability of loan statistics to measure and project library use, service to groups of library users may be improved. The current loan transaction indicates what is happening and there by may allow the library's administration to respond to the demands of the library's users as deduced from the loan statistics.

If a definitive pattern can be obtained about how effective

the library is in meeting user requirements, far more precise parameters of library service may be established. A further illustration of the total systems concept is the loan transaction record accumulated over a period of time; this could be very meaningful in arriving at staff subject specialist requirements.

The nature of the user, derived from subject profile analyses by questionnaire and personal interviews as well as from actual use reports, would provide a guide to the subject background and experience needed for meeting the needs of the library's community. Although this would be only a partial measurement, it would still contribute to a broader understanding of job requirements.

Recent Development: Online Applications

The analyst in designing a system utilizing the total systems concept not only should be aware of what effect the design will have on other systems but also should be cognizant of and prepared for new technological developments. A computer-based circulation system should be designed to take into account on-line operating proce-dures. By an on-line operation is meant direct input to the computer, usually with immediate response from the computer. Printouts may still be used as guides to the out-standing circulation. An on-line procedure makes unnecessary the preparation of the computer input, the transaction card of the master book card's data combined with user's identification. This transaction data goes directly into the computer storage. In an on-line application with immediate access, loan information will not only go directly to the computer but also, as requested, will be printed out on a typewriter terminal or displayed on a cathode-ray tube.

METADATA

Meta is a classical Greek preposition and prefix conveying the following senses in English, depending upon the case of the associated noun: among; along with; with; by means of; in the midst of; after; behind. In epistemology, the word means "about (its own category)"; thus metadata is "data about the data". The term was introduced intuitively, without a formal definition. Because of that, today there are various definitions. The most common one is the literal translation: "Data about data are referred to as metadata."

Example: "12345" is data, and with no additional context is meaningless. When "12345" is given a meaningful name (metadata) of "ZIP code", one can understand , and further placing "ZIP code" within the context of a postal address) that "12345" refers to the General Electric plant in Schenectady, New York.

As for most people the difference between data and information is merely a philosophical one of no relevance in practical use, other definitions are:

(a) Metadata is information about data.

(b) Metadata is information about information.

(c) Metadata contains information about that data or other data

There are more sophisticated definitions, such as:

1. "Metadata is structured, encoded data that describe characteristics of information-bearing entities to aid in the identification, discovery, assessment, and management of the described entities."
2. "[Metadata is a set of] optional structured descriptions that are publicly available to explicitly assist in locating objects."

These are used more rarely because they tend to concentrate on one purpose of metadata — to find "objects", "entities" or "resources" — and ignore others, such as using metadata to optimize compression algorithms, or to perform additional computations using the data. The metadata concept has been extended into the world of systems to include any "data about data": the names of tables, columns, programs, and the like. Different views of this "system metadata" are detailed below, but beyond that is the recognition that metadata can describe all aspects of systems: data, activities, people and organizations involved, locations of data and processes, access methods, limitations, timing and events, as well as motivation and rules. Fundamentally, then, metadata is "the data that describe the structure and workings of an organization's use of information, and which describe the systems it uses to manage that information". To do a model of metadata is to do an "Enterprise model" of the information technology industry itself.

Objective

Metadata provides context for data. Metadata is used to facilitate the understanding, usage, and management of data, both by human and computers. Thus metadata can describe the data conceptually so that others can understand them; it can describe the data syntactically so others can use them; and the two types of descriptions together can facilitate decisions about how to manage the data. The metadata required to effectively work with data varies with the type of data, their context of use, and their purpose. Often data providers will provide users access to a variety of metadata fields, which can be used individually or in combinations, and applied by different users to achieve different goals. These users can be human 'end users', or other computing systems.

When structured into a hierarchical arrangement, metadata is more properly called an ontology or schema. Both terms describe "what exists" for some purpose or to enable some action. For instance, the arrangement of subject headings in a library catalog serves not only as a guide to finding books on a particular subject in the stacks, but also as a guide to what subjects "exist" in the library's own ontology and how more specialized topics are related to or derived from the more general subject headings. Metadata is frequently stored in a central location and used to help organizations standardize their data. This information is typically stored in a metadata registry.

These examples list metadata that describe particular digital entities. For clarity and consistency with some definitions of metadata, these examples are expressed with respect to digitized form of each entity, not data that is represented solely in a physical object like a book. (For information resources that are not in digital form, metadata is only the information that describes the information content, not the information about the physical representation.) In most cases, the examples illustrate the use of metadata to describe the entity's content (conceptually), how the entity came to be (provenance), and information necessary for the system to use it. The last set of information about system-related details is typically hidden from the user, but includes the internal file name, location, and creation/access times for the digital entity. Because the concept of metadata is specific to each situation—"one person's data is another person's metadata"—examples should be considered illustrative rather than absolute.

Examples of metadata regarding a book would be the title, author(s), date of publication, subject, a unique identifier (such as International Standard Book Number (ISBN)), number of pages, and the language of the text. Metadata unique to the electronic format includes usage (last opened, current page, times read) and other user-provided data (ranking, tags, annotations). System use metadata might include purchase and digital rights information for the content.

Digital images include both digital photographs, and images

that have been created or modified on a computer. Metadata for a digital photograph typically includes the date and time at which it was created and details of the camera settings (such as focal length, aperture, exposure). Many digital cameras record metadata in their digital images, in formats like exchangeable image file format (EXIF) or JPEG. Some cameras can automatically include extended metadata such as the location the picture was taken (e.g., from a GPS). Most image editing software includes at least some metadata in the digital image, and can include content about the image's provenance and licensing.

Audio recordings may also be labeled with metadata. When audio formats moved from analogue to digital, it became possible to embed this metadata within the digital content itself. (Without any metadata, the digital content is simply a file containing the audio waveform.) Metadata can be used to name, describe, catalogue and indicate ownership or copyright for a digital audio file, as well as allow user characterizations of the audio content (ratings, tags, and other auxiliary metadata). Its presence simplifies locating a specific audio file within a group, through use of a search engine that accesses the metadata. The typical audio player or audio application on a computer relies heavily on metadata to provide user features.

As different digital audio formats were developed, it was agreed that a standardized and specific location would be set aside within the digital files where this information could be stored. As a result, almost all digital audio formats, including mp3, broadcast wav and AIFF files, have similar standardized locations that can be populated with metadata. This "information about information" has become one of the great advantages of working with digital audio files, since the catalogue and descriptive information that makes up the metadata is built right into the audio file itself, ready for easy access and use.

The HTML format used to define web pages allows for the inclusion of a variety of types of metadata, from simple descriptive text, dates and keywords to highly-granular information such as the Dublin Core and e-GMS standards. Pages can be geotagged with coordinates. Metadata may be included in the page's header or in a separate file. Microformats allow metadata to be added to on-page data in a way that users don't see, but computers can readily access.

Levels

The hierarchy of metadata descriptions can go on forever, but usually context or semantic understanding makes extensively detailed explanations unnecessary.

The role played by any particular datum depends on the context. For example, when considering the geography of London, "E8 3BJ" would be a datum and "Post Code" would be metadatum. But, when considering the data management of an automated system that manages geographical data, "Post Code" might be a datum and then "data item name" and "6 characters, starting with A–Z" would be metadata.

In any particular context, metadata characterizes the data it describes, not the entity described by that data. So, in relation to "E8 3BJ", the datum "is in London" is a further description of the place in the real world which has the post code "E8 3BJ", not of the code itself. Therefore, although it is providing information connected to "E8 3BJ" (telling us that this is the post code of a place in London), this would not normally be considered metadata, as it is describing "E8 3BJ" as a place in the real world and not as data.

Markup

In the context of the web and the work of the W3C in providing markup technologies of HTML, XML and SGML the concept of metadata has specific context that is perhaps clearer than in other information domains. With markup technologies there is metadata, markup and data content. The metadata describes characteristics about the data, while the markup identifies the specific type of data content and acts as a container for that document instance. This page in Wikipedia is itself an example of such usage, where the textual information is data, how it is packaged, linked, referenced, styled and displayed is markup and aspects and characteristics of that markup are metadata set globally across Wikipedia. In the context of markup the metadata is architected to allow optimization of document instances to contain only a minimum amount of metadata, while the metadata itself is likely referenced externally such as in a schema definition (XSD) instance. Also it should be noted that markup provides specialised mechanisms that handle referential data, again avoiding confusion over what is metadata or data, and allowing optimizations. The reference and ID mechanisms in markup allowing reference links between related data items, and links to data items that can then be repeated about a data item, such as an address or product details. These are then all themselves simply more data items and markup instances rather than metadata.

Similarly there are concepts such as classifications, ontologies and associations for which markup mechanisms are provided. A data item can then be linked to such categories via markup and hence provide a clean delineation between what is metadata, and actual data instances. Therefore the concepts and descriptions in a classification would be metadata, but the actual classification entry for a data item is simply another data instance.

Some examples can illustrate the points here. Items in bold are data content, in italic are metadata, normal text items are all markup.

The two examples show in-line use of metadata within markup relating to a data instance (XML) compared to simple markup (HTML).

A simple HTML instance example:

```
<span style="normalText">Example</span>
```

And then an XML instance example with metadata:

```
<PersonMiddleName nillable="true">John</PersonMiddleName>
```

Where the inline assertion that a person's middle name may be an empty data item is metadata about the data item. Such definitions however are usually not placed inline in XML. Instead these definitions are moved away into the schema definition that contains the metadata for the entire document instance. This again illustrates another important aspect of metadata in the context of markup. The metadata is optimally defined only once for a collection of data instances. Hence repeated items of markup are rarely metadata, but rather more markup data instances themselves.

Difference between Data and Metadata

Usually it is not possible to distinguish between (plain) data and metadata because:

1. Something can be data and metadata at the same time. The headline of an article is both its title (metadata) and part of its text (data).
2. Data and metadata can change their roles. A poem, as such, would be regarded as data, but if there is a song that uses it as lyrics, the whole poem could be attached to an audio file of the song as metadata. Thus, the labeling depends on the point of view.

These considerations apply no matter which of the above

definitions is considered, except where explicit markup is used to denote what is data and what is metadata.

Use

Metadata has many different applications; this section lists some of the most common.

Metadata is used to speed up and enrich searching for resources. In general, search queries using metadata can save users from performing more complex filter operations manually. It is now common for web browsers (with the notable exception of Mozilla Firefox), P2P applications and media management software to automatically download and locally cache metadata, to improve the speed at which files can be accessed and searched. Metadata may also be associated to files manually. This is often the case with documents which are scanned into a document storage repository such as FileNet or Documentum. Once the documents have been converted into an electronic format a user brings the image up in a viewer application, manually reads the document and keys values into an online application to be stored in a metadata repository.

Metadata helps to bridge the semantic gap. By telling a computer how data items are related and how these relations can be evaluated automatically, it becomes possible to process even more complex filter and search operations. For example, if a search engine understands that "Van Gogh" was a "Dutch painter", it can answer a search query on "Dutch painters" with a link to a web page about Vincent Van Gogh, although the exact words "Dutch painters" never occur on that page. This approach, called knowledge representation, is of special interest to the semantic web and artificial intelligence. Certain metadata is designed to optimize lossy compression. For example, if a video has metadata that allows a computer to tell foreground from background, the latter can be compressed more aggressively to achieve a higher compression rate.

Some metadata is intended to enable variable content presentation. For example, if a picture has metadata that indicates the most important region — the one where there is a person — an image viewer on a small screen, such as on a mobile phone's, can narrow the picture to that region and thus show the user the most interesting details. A similar kind of metadata is intended to allow blind people to access diagrams and pictures, by converting them for special output devices or reading their description using text-to-speech software. Other descriptive metadata can be used to automate workflows. For example, if a "smart" software tool knows content and structure of data, it can convert it automatically and pass it to another "smart" tool as input. As a result, users save the many copy-and-paste operations required when analyzing data with "dumb" tools.

Metadata is becoming an increasingly important part of electronic discovery. Application and file system metadata derived from electronic documents and files can be important evidence. Recent changes to the Federal Rules of Civil Procedure make metadata routinely discoverable as part of civil litigation. Parties to litigation are required to maintain and produce metadata as part of discovery, and spoliation of metadata can lead to sanctions. Metadata has become important on the World Wide Web because of the need to find useful information from the mass of information available. Manually-created metadata adds value because it ensures consistency. If a web page about a certain topic contains a word or phrase, then all web pages about that topic should contain that same word or phrase. Metadata also ensures variety, so that if a topic goes by two names each will be used. For example, an article about "sport utility vehicles" would also be tagged "4 wheel drives", "4WDs" and "four wheel drives", as this is how SUVs are known in some countries. Examples of metadata for an audio CD include the MusicBrainz project and All Media Guide's Allmusic. Similarly, MP3 files have metadata tags in a format called ID3.

GLOSSARY

AACR2 (Anglo-American Cataloguing Rules)

A set of rules that describe the content that is contained in library catalog records.

Abstracting and Indexing Services

Secondary information services that provide searching of scholarly and scientific information, in particular of individual journal articles.

Access Management

Control of access to material in digital libraries. Sometimes called terms and conditions or rights management.

ACM Digital Library

A digital library of the journals and conference proceedings published by the Association for Computing Machinery.

Alexandria Digital Library

A digital library of geospatial information, based at the University of California, Santa Barbara.

American Memory and the National Digital Library Programme

The Library of Congress's digital library of materials converted from its primary source materials related to American history.

Applet

A small computer programme that can be transmitted from a server to a client computer and executed on the client.

Archives

Collections with related systems and services, organized to emphasize the long-term preservation of information.

Art and Architecture Thesaurus

A controlled vocabulary for fine art, architecture, decorative art, and material culture, a project of the J. Paul Getty Trust.

Artifact

A physical object in a library, archive, or museum.

ASCII (American Standard Code for Information Interchange)

A coding scheme that represents individual characters as 7 or 8 bits; printable ASCII is a subset of ASCII.

Authentication

Validation of a user, a computer, or some digital object to ensure that it is what is claims to be.

Authorization

Giving permission to a user or client computer to access specific information and carry out approved actions.

Automatic Indexing

Creation of catalog or indexing records using computer programmes, not human cataloguers.

Boolean Searching

Methods of information retrieval where a query consists of a sequence of search terms, combined with operators, such as "and", "or", and "not".

Browser

A general-purpose user interface, used with the web and other online information services. Also known as a web browser.

Browsing

Exploration of a body of information, based on the organization of the collections or scanning lists, rather than by direct searching.

Cache

A temporary store that is used to keep a readily available copy of recently used data or any data that is expected to be used frequently.

California Digital Library

A digital library that serves the nine campuses of the University of California.

Catalog

A collection of bibliographic records created according to an established set of rules.

Classification

An organization of library materials by a hierarchy of subject categories.

Client

A computer that acts on behalf of a user, including a user's personal computer, or another computer that appears to a server to have that function.

CGI (Common Gateway Interface)

A programming interface that enables a web browser to be an interface to information services other than web sites.

Chemical Abstracts

A secondary information service for chemistry.

CNI (Coalition for Networked Information)

A partnership of the Association for Research Libraries and Educause to collaborate on academic networked information.

Complex Object

Library object that is made up from many inter-related elements or digital objects.

Compression

Reduction in the size of digital materials by removing redundancy or by approximation; lossless compression can be reversed; lossy compression can not be reversed since information is lost by approximation.

Controlled Vocabulary

A set of subject terms, and rules for their use in assigning terms to materials for indexing and retrieval.

Conversion

Transformation of information from one medium to another, including from paper to digital form.

CORBA

A standard for distributed computing where an object on one computer invokes an Object Request Broker (ORB) to interact with an object on another computer.

CORE

A project from 1991 to 1995 by Bellcore, Cornell University, OCLC, and the American Chemical Society to convert chemistry journals to digital form.

Cryptolope

Secure container used to buy and sell content securely over the Internet, developed by IBM.

CSS (Cascading Style Sheets)

System of style sheets for use with HTML, the basis of XLS.

CSTR (Computer Science Technical Reports Project)

A DARPA-funded research project with CNRI and five universities, from 1992 to 1996.

DARPA (Defense Advanced Research Projects Agency)

A major sponsor of computer science research in the U.S., including digital libraries. Formerly ARPA.

Data Type

Structural metadata associated with digital data that indicates the digital format or the application used to process the data.

DES (Data Encryption Standard)

A method for private key encryption.

Desktop Metaphor

User interface concept on personal computers that represents information as files and folders on a desktop.

Dienst

An architecture for digital library services and an open protocol that provides those services, developed at Cornell University, used in NCSTRL.

Digital Archeology

The process of retrieving information from damaged, fragmentary, and archaic data sources.

Digital Libraries Initiative

A digital libraries research programme. In Phase 1, from 1994 to 1998, NSF/DARPA/NASA funded six university projects Phase 2 began in 1998/9.

Digital Object

An item as stored in a digital library, consisting of data, metadata, and an identifier.

Digital Signature

A cryptographic code consisting of a hash, to indicate that data has not changed, that can be decrypted with the public key of the creator of the signature.

Dissemination

The transfer from the stored form of a digital object in a repository to a client.

Distributed Computing

Computing systems in which services to users are provided by teams of computers collaborating over a network.

D-Lib Magazine

A monthly, online publication about digital libraries research and innovation.

DLITE

An experimental user interface used with the Stanford University InfoBus.

Document

Digital object that is the analog of a physical document, especially textual materials; a document model is an object model for documents.

Domain Name

The name of a computer on the Internet; the domain name service (DNS) converts domain names to IP addresses.

DOI (Digital Object Identifier)

An identifier used by publishers to identify materials published electronically, a form of handle.

DSSSL (Document Style Semantics and Specification Language)

A general purpose system of style sheets for SGML.

DTD (Document Type Definition)

A mark-up specification for a class of documents, defined within the SGML framework.

Dublin Core

A simple set of metadata elements used in digital libraries, primarily to describe digital objects and for collections management, and for exchange of metadata.

Dynamic Object

Digital object where the dissemination presented to the user depends upon the execution of a computer programme, or other external activity.

EAD (Encoded Archival Description)

A DTD used to encode electronic versions of finding aids for archival materials.

Electronic Journal

A online publication that is organized like a traditional printed journal, either an online version of a printed journal or a journal that has only an online existence.

ELib

A British programme of innovation, around the theme of electronic publication.

Emulation

Replication of a computing system to process programmes and data from an early system that is no longer available.

Encryption

Techniques for encoding information for privacy or security, so that it appears to be random data; the reverse process, decryption, requires knowledge of a digital key.

Entities and Elements

In a mark-up language, entities are the basic unit of information, including character entities; elements are strings of entities that form a structural unit.

Expression

The realization of a work, by expressing the abstract concept as actual words, sounds, images, etc.

Fair Use

A concept in copyright law that allows limited use of copyright material without requiring permission from the rights holders, e.g., for scholarship or review.

Federated Digital Library

A group of digital libraries that support common standards and services, thus providing interoperability and a coherent service to users.

Field, Subfield

An individual item of information in a structured record, such as a catalog or database record.

Fielded Searching

Methods for searching textual materials, including catalogs, where search terms are matched against the content of specified fields.

Finding Aid

A textual document that describes holdings of an archive, library, or museum.

Firewall

A computer system that screens data passing between network segments, used to provide security for a private network at the point of connection to the Internet.

First Sale

A concept in copyright law that permits the purchaser of a book or other object to transfer it to somebody else, without requiring permission from the rights holders.

FTP (File Transfer Protocol)

A protocol used to transmit files between computers on the Internet.

Full Text Searching

Methods for searching textual materials where the entire text is matched against a query.

Gatherer

A programme that automatically assembles indexing information from digital library collections.

Gazetteer

A database used to translate between different representations of geospatial references, such as place names and geographic coordinates.

Genre

The class or category of an object when considered as an intellectual work.

Geospatial Information

Information that is reference by a geographic location.

Google

A web search programme that ranks web pages in a list of hits by giving weight to the links that reference a specific page.

Gopher

A pre-web protocol used for building digital libraries, now largely obsolete.

Handle

A system of globally-unique names for Internet resources and a computer system for managing them, developed by CNRI; a form of URN.

Harvest

A research project that developed an architecture for distributed searching, including protocols and formats.

Hash

A short value calculated from digital data that serves to distinguish it from other data.

HTML (Hyper-Text Mark-up Language)

A simple mark-up and formatting language for text, with links to other objects, used with the web.

HTTP (Hyper-Text Transport Protocol)

The basic protocol of the web, used for communication between browsers and web sites.

Hyperlink

A network link from one item in a digital library or web site to another.

ICPSR (International Consortium for Political and Social Science Research)

An archive of social science datasets, based at the University of Michigan.

Identifier

A string of characters that identifies a specific resource in a digital library or on a network.

ETF (Internet Engineering Task Force)

The body that coordinates the technological development of the Internet, including standards.

InfoBus

An approach to interoperability that uses proxies as interfaces between existing systems, developed at Stanford University.

Information Discovery

General term covering all strategies and methods of finding information in a digital library.

Information Retrieval

Searching a body of information for objects that match a search query.

Informedia

A research programme and digital library of segments of video, based at Carnegie Mellon University.

Inspec

An indexing service for physics, engineering, computer science, and related fields.

Internet

An international network, consisting of independently managed networks using the TCP/IP protocols and a shared naming system. A successor to the ARPAnet.

Internet RFC Series

The technical documentation of the Internet, provided by the Internet Engineering Task Force. Internet Drafts are preliminary versions of RFCs.

Interoperability

The task of building coherent services for users from components that are technically different and independently managed.

Inverted File

A list of the words in a set of documents and their locations within those documents; an inverted list is the list of locations for a given word.

Item

A specific piece of material in a digital library; a single instance or copy of a manifestation.

Java

A programming language used for writing mobile code, especially for user interfaces, developed by Sun Microsystems.

JavaScript

A scripting language used to embed executable instructions in a web page.

JPEG

A format for storing compressed images.

JSTOR

A subscription service, initiated by the Andrew W. Mellon Foundation, to convert back runs of important journals and make them available to academic libraries.

Key

A digital code used to encrypt or decrypt messages. Private key encryption uses a single, secret key. Dual key (public key) encryption uses two keys of which one is secret and one is public.

Legacy System

An existing system, usually a computer system, that must be accommodated in building new systems.

Lexicon

A linguistic tool with information about the morphological variations and grammatical usage of words.

Lexis

A legal information service, a pioneer of full-text information online.

Los Alamos E-Print Archives

An open-access site for rapid distribution of research papers in physics and related disciplines.

Manifestation

Form given to an expression of a work, e.g., by representing it in digital form.

MARC (Machine-Readable Cataloging)

A format used by libraries to store and exchange catalog records.

Mark-up Language

Codes embedded in a document that describe its structure and/or its format.

Medline

An indexing service for research in medicine and related fields, provided by the National Library of Medicine.

MELVYL

A shared digital library system for academic institutions in California; part of the California Digital Library.

Memex

A concept of an online library suggested by Vannevar Bush in 1945.

Mercury

An experimental digital library project to mount scientific journals online at Carnegie Mellon University from 1987 to 1993.

MeSH (Medical Subject Headings)

A set of subject term and associated thesaurus used to describe medical research, maintained by the National Library of Medicine.

Metadata

Data about other data, commonly divided into descriptive metadata such as bibliographic information, structural metadata about formats and structures, and administrative metadata, which is used to manage information.

Migration

Preservation of digital content, where the underlying information is retained but older formats and internal structures are replaced by newer.

MIME (Internet Media Type)

A scheme for specifying the data type of digital material.

Mirror

A computer system that contains a duplicate copy of information stored in another system.

Mobile Code

Computer programmes or parts of programmes that are transmitted across a network and executed by a remote computer.

Morphology

Grammatical and other variants of words that are derived from the same root or stem.

Mosaic

The first widely-used web browser, developed at the University of Illinois.

MPEG

A family of formats for compressing and storing digitized video and sound.

Multimedia

A combination of several media types in a single digital object or collection, e.g., images, audio, video.

Natural Language Processing

Use of computers to interpret and manipulate words as part of a language.

NCSTRL (Networked Computer Science Technical Reports Library)

An international distributed library of computer science materials and services, based at Cornell University.

Netlib

A digital library of mathematical software and related collections.

NSF (National Science Foundation)

U.S. government agency that supports science and engineering, including digital libraries research.

Object

A technical computing term for an independent piece of computer code with its data. Hence, object-oriented programming, and distributed objects, where objects are connected over a network.

Object Model

A description of the structural relationships among components of a library object including its metadata.

OCLC (Online Computer Library System)

An organization that provides, among other services, a bibliographic utility for libraries to share catalog records.

OPAC (Online Public Access Catalog)

An online library catalog used by library patrons.

Open Access

Resources that are openly available to users with no requirements for authentication or payment.

Optical Character Recognition

Automatic conversion of text from a digitized image to computer text.

Pad++

A experimental user interface for access to large collections of information, based on semantic zooming.

Page Description Language

A system for encoding documents that precisely describes their appearance when rendered for printing or display.

PDF (Portable Document Format)

A page description language developed by Adobe Corporation to store and render images of pages.

Peer Review

The procedure by which academic journal articles are reviewed by other researchers before being accepted for publication.

Perseus

A digital library of hyperlinked sources in classics and related disciplines, based at Tufts University.

Policy

A rule established by the manager of a digital library that specifies which users should be authorized to have what access to which materials.

Port

A method used by TCP to specify which programme running on a computer should process a message arriving over the Internet.

PostScript

A programming language to create graphical output for printing, used as a page description language.

Precision

In information retrieval, the percentage of hits found by a search that satisfy the request that generated the query.

Presentation Profile

Guidelines associated with a digital object that suggest how it might be presented to a user.

Protocol

A set of rules that describe the sequence of messages sent across a network, specifying both syntax and semantics.

Proxy

A computer that acts as a bridge between two computer systems that use different standards, formats, or protocols.

Publish

To make information available and distribute it to the public.

PURL (Persistent URL)

A method of providing persistent identifiers using standard web protocols, developed by OCLC.

Query

A textual string, possibly structured, that is used in information retrieval, the task being to find objects that match the words in the query.

Ranked Searching

Methods of information retrieval that return a list of documents, ranked in order of how well each matches the query,

RDF (Resource Description Framework)

A method for specifying the syntax of metadata, used to exchange metadata.

RealAudio

A format and protocol for compressing and storing digitized

sound, and transmitting it over a network to be played in real time.

Recall

In informational retrieval, the percentage of the items in a body of material which would satisfy a request that are actually found by a search.

Refresh

To make an exact copy of data from older media to newer for long-term preservation.

Render

To transform digital information in the form received from a repository into a display on a computer screen, or for other presentation to the user.

Replication

Make copies of digital material for backup, performance, reliability, or preservation.

Repository

A computer system used to store digital library collections and disseminate them to users.

RSA Encryption

A method of dual key (public key) encryption.

Scanning

Method of conversion in which a physical object, e.g., a printed page, is represented by a digital grid of pixels

Search Term

A single term within a query, usually a single word or short phrase.

Secondary Information

Information sources that describe other (primary) information, e.g., catalogs, indexes, and abstracts; used to find information and manage collections.

Security

Techniques and practices that preserve the integrity of computer systems, and digital library services and collections.

Server

Any computer on a network, other than a client, that stores collections or provides services.

SGML (Standard Generalized Markup Language)

A system for creating mark-up languages that represent the structure of a document.

SICI (Serial Item and Contribution Identifier)

An identifier for an issue of a serial or an article contained within a serial.

Speech Recognition

Automatic conversion of spoken words to computer text.

STARTS

An experimental protocol for use in distributed searching, which enables a client to combine results from several search engines.

Stemming

In informational retrieval, reduction of morphological variants of a word to a common stem.

Stop Word

A word that is so common that it is ignored in information retrieval. A set of such words is called a stop list.

Structural Type

Metadata that indicates the structural category of a digital object.

Style Sheet

A set of rules that specify how mark-up in a document translates into the appearance of the document when rendered.

Subscription

In a digital library, a payment made by a person or an organization for access to specific collections and services, usually for a fixed period, e.g., one year.

Subsequent Use

Use made of digital materials after they leave the control of a digital library.

Tag

A special string of characters embedded in marked-up text to indicate the structure or format.

TCP/IP

The base protocols of the Internet. IP uses numeric IP addresses to join network segments; TCP provides reliable delivery of messages between networked computers.

TEI (Text Encoding Initiative)

A project to represent texts in digital form, emphasizing the needs of humanities scholars. Also the DTD used by the programme.

TeX

A method of encoding text that precisely describes its appearance when printed, especially good for mathematical notation. LaTeX is a version of TeX.

Thesaurus

A linguistic tool that relates words by meaning.

Ticer Summer School

A programme at Tilburg University to educate experienced librarians about digital libraries.

Tipster

A DARPA programme of research to improve the quality of text processing methods, including information retrieval.

Transliteration

A systematic way to convert characters in one alphabet or phonetic sounds into another alphabet.

TREC (Text Retrieval Conferences)

Annual conferences in which methods of text processing are evaluated against standard collections and tasks.

Truncation

Use of the first few letters of a word as a search term in information retrieval.

Tulip

An experiment in which Elsevier Science scanned material science journals and a group of universities mounted them on local computers.

UDP

An Internet protocol which transmits data packets without error checking.

Unicode

A 16-bit code to represent the characters used in most of the world's scripts. UTF-8 is an alternative encoding in which one or more 8-bit bytes represents each Unicode character.

Union Catalog

A single catalog that contains records about materials in several collections or libraries.

URL (Uniform Resource Locator)

A reference to a resource on the Internet, specifying a protocol, a computer, a file on that computer, and parameters.

An absolute URL specifies a location as a domain name or IP address; a relative URL specifies a location relative to the current file.

URN (Uniform Resource Name)

Location-independent names for Internet resources.

WAIS

An early version of Z39.50, used in digital libraries before the web, now largely obsolete.

Warwick Framework

A general model that describes the various parts of a complex object, including the various categories of metadata.

Watermark

A code embedded into digital material that can be used to establish ownership, may be visible or invisible to the user.

Web crawler

A web indexing programme that builds an index by following hyperlinks continuously from web page to web page.

Webmaster

A person who manages web sites.

Web Search Services

Commercial services that provide searching of the web, including: Yahoo, Altavista, Excite, Lycos, Infoseek, etc.

Web Site

A collection of information on the web; usually stored on a web server.

Westlaw

A legal information service provided by West Publishing.

World Wide Web (Web)

An interlinked set of information sources on the Internet, and the technology they use, including HTML, HTTP, URLs, and MIME.

Work

The underlying intellectual abstraction behind some material in a digital library.

Xerox Digital Property Rights Language

Syntax and rules for expressing rights, conditions, and fees for digital works.

XLS (eXtensible Style Language)

System of style sheets for use with XML, derived from CSS.

Bibliography

Breeding, Marshall. "Preserving Digital Information." *Information Today* 19: 5, 2002.

Bretherton, F. P. and Singley, P. T. 1994, Metadata: A User's View, *Proceedings of the International Conference on Very Large Data Bases* (VLDB), 1091-1094.

Burman, J.S., *Computers in Libraries,* Rajat, New Delhi, 2007.

Cain, Mark. "Managing Technology: Being a Library of Record in a Digital Age", *Journal of Academic Librarianship* 29: 6, 2003.

Carol Tenopir and Donald King (2000). *Towards Electronic Journals.* Special Libraries Association.

Committee on Institutional Cooperation: Partnership announced between CIC and Google, 6 June 2007, Retrieved 7 July 2007.

Computer Readable Databases: A Directory and Data Source Book 6th ed. 1990 Gale Research Inc. Detroit.

Doctorow, Cory (2004). Ebooks: Neither E, Nor Books, *O'Reilly Emerging Technologies Conference.*

Edward A. Fox. The Digital Libraries Initiative - Update and Discussion, *Bulletin of the American Society of Information Science*, Vol. 26, No 1, October/November 1999.

European Commission steps up efforts to put Europe's memory on the Web via a "European Digital Library" Europa press release, 2 March 2006.

Flint, Eric (2000). "Building the Baen Free Library". http: // www.speculations.com/?t=189167.

Garudadwajan, B. and Subramanya, H.S. Dedicated line-European Space Agency Database NAL's experience. Paper presented at National Seminar on modes of Access to online databases and application of CD-ROM and other optical discs - NAL and AGLIS, Bangalore 27-29 June 1988.

Gertz, J., 2000 April, Selection for preservation in the digital age: An overview. *Library Resources & Technical Services,* 44(2), 97-104.

Gertz, Janet. "Selection for Preservation in the Digital Age." *Library Resources & Technical Services.* 44(2), 2000: 97-104.

Gonçalves, M.A., Fox, E.A., Watson, L.T., & Kipp, N.A. (2004). Streams, Structures, Spaces, Scenarios, Societies (5S): A Formal Model for Digital Libraries. ACM Transactions on Information Systems (TOIS), 22 (2), 270-312.

Government of India, Ministry of Science and Technology, Department of Scientific and Industrial Research - National Information System for Science and Technology (NISSAT) Detailed Project Report (1985-90) pp. 7-8,47-49.

Greenstein, Daniel I., Thorin, Suzanne Elizabeth. *The Digital Library: A Biography.* Digital Library Federation, 2002.

Harter, Stephen P. *Online Information Retrieval Concepts Principles and Techniques.* Academic Press, 1986.

Heritage Preservation, 2005. *A Public Trust at Risk: The Heritage Health Index Report on the State of America's Collections.* Washington, D.C.: Heritage Preservation.

Hoberman, Steve, *Data Modeling Made Simple*, 2nd Edition, Technics Publications, LLC, 2009.

Jacob Hiller (2008). How authors can take advatange of ebooks., *The Automated Ebook*.

James Martin, Strategic Data Planning Methodologies, Prentice-Hall, Inc., Englewood Cliffs, New Jersey, 1982.

James, Bradley (2002). The Electronic Book: Looking Beyond the Physical Codex, *SciNet*.

Kahn, R.E., & Cerf, V.G. (1988). The Digital Library Project Volume I: The World of Knowbots, (DRAFT): An Open Architecture For a Digital Library System and a Plan For Its Development. Reston, VA: Corporation for National Research Initiatives.

Koehler, AEC. *Some Thoughts on the Meaning of Open Access for University Library Technical Services* Serials Review Vol. 32, 1, 2006, p. 17.

Kumar, S., *Digital Library Development,* Rajat, New Delhi, 2009.

L. Candela et al., *The DELOS Digital Library Reference Model - Foundations for Digital Libraries*. Version 0.98, February 2008.

Levy, D.M. & Marshall, C.C. (1995.) Going digital: A look at assumptions underlying digital libraries. Communications of the ACM, 38(4), 77-84.

Liddell & Scott, *An Intermediate Greek-English Lexicon,* OUP.

Lynch, Clifford (2001). The Battle to Define the Future of the Book in the Digital World, *First Monday - Peer reviewed journal on the Internet*.

Menta, Robert (2000). Read an e-book to your child, go to jail?, *MP3 Newswire*.

Outline of DELOS Joint Programme of Activities (JPA) from the Technical Annex to the DELOS contract, which was approved by the European Commission in December 2003.

Pastore, Michael (2008). 30 Benefits of Ebooks, *Epublishers Weekly*.

Pymm, Bob. "Building Collections for All Time: The Issue of Significance." *Australian Academic & Research Libraries.* 37(1) 2006: 61-73.

Robertson, S., Jitan, S., & Reese, K. (1997). Web-based collaborative library research. *Proceedings of the 2nd ACM International Conference on Digital Libraries*, 152-160.

Silipigni Connaway, L, et al., 2006, July. Last copies: What's at risk? *College & Research Libraries*, 67(4), 370-9.

Stanford Copyright & Fair Use - Digital Preservation and Copyright by Peter B. Hirtle.

Teper, Thomas H. "Where Next? Long-Term Considerations for Digital Initiatives." *Kentucky Libraries* 65(2), 2000: 12-18.

Torpie, Geraldine. Going online 1988. *Aslib* 1987.

Verma, K., *ICTs in Libraries*, Akansha, New Delhi, 2004.

Verma, K., *Digital Library Preservation Strategies*, Akansha, New Delhi, 2005.

William R. Durrell, *Data Administration: A Practical Guide to Data Administration*, McGraw-Hill, 1985.

Index